SOLDIERS
SOLDIERS

SOLDIERS
SOLDIERS

RICHARD BOWOOD

PAUL HAMLYN • LONDON

CONTENTS

Edited by Derek Lord
Designed by John Hawkins
Published by PAUL HAMLYN LTD
Westbook House Fulham Broadway London
© Copyright 1965 Paul Hamlyn Ltd
Printed in Czechoslovakia by Polygrafia, Prague
T 1459

ABOUT THIS BOOK

The dictionary defines a soldier as: "one who serves in an army for pay; one who takes part in military service or warfare". So the soldier is one who *serves*. He is set apart from the civilian by discipline and obedience to his superiors, and serves for the safety or benefit of the civilian.

The soldier is a man who has made a contract, either voluntarily, or through necessity caused by a national emergency, or because he is conscripted by law. By that contract, he undertakes to obey orders and, when so commanded, to fight his country's enemies, even to the death. In return, he is paid, clothed, fed and housed.

War is a disaster, battle is beastly; but it is not the soldier who causes war and commits men to battle. The soldier only wages the war others have caused, and fights the battles for them. One can condemn war, but it would be unfair to condemn with it the soldier.

He may fight from a sense of duty, or perhaps only because he has been trained for that purpose; he might fight from a sense of honour and justice, or because he will not fail his comrades. Even though warfare is essentially evil, the cause may be good and the courage of the fighting man may be sublime. In battle, a man can often attain the heights of heroism and self-sacrifice.

Soldiers are men to be respected and honoured, though they have not always been of the most respectable kind. The Duke of Wellington once described his army as the scum of the earth. But, on another occasion, he said: "The best troops, the best troops in the world, are the British Infantry". Always, in the Assyrian hosts, in the Roman legions, in the armies of Charlemagne, Frederick the Great, Napoleon—in every army—there have been rogues and rascals, and honest men whose sole desire was to serve their country. Each kind has produced its heroes.

In this book we take a glance at soldiers of all ages and nations, at the conditions of service, the tactics, weapons and customs. The range is wide and details greatly differ. Yet certain common qualities can be discerned— loyalty, esprit-de-corps and, always, the comradeship which is inseparable from service life. Above all, the soldiers of every age and of every race have had one duty in common: to stand in the forefront of the battle and fight to the death.

SOLDIERS
OF LONG AGO

The little knowledge we have of Early Man comes from tools and weapons found in the ground, and drawings and paintings on the walls of caves. Most of the cave drawings depict hunting scenes, but in Spain there are pictures of warriors which were drawn before history was recorded, and these may be our earliest soldiers.

The earliest detailed evidence of military organisation comes from the fertile valleys of the Tigris and Euphrates, now Iraq, and from the Nile valley. Archaeologists have discovered weapons and military equipment, paintings in temples and tombs, and written accounts, which tell us about armies of six and seven thousand years ago.

SUMERIAN SOLDIERS

The oldest civilisation we know about is the Sumerian, the race which lived in and around the city of Ur, south of the Euphrates and near the Persian Gulf. Ur, said to have been the home of Abraham, was a wealthy civilisation some four thousand years before Christ, and it seems to have had a well-organised army. Royal tombs at Ur have yielded much treasure and information. When the king died, his court was buried with him, and apparently the unfortunate courtiers went to the tomb willingly. Sixty-three bodies were found in one royal tomb, sixty-eight in another and seventy-four in a third. The bodies were arranged about the royal coffin in order, and among them were soldiers. In one tomb, eight soldiers lay in a double rank, with spears and helmets, and others were beside the king's chariot.

In the tombs were gold vessels, fine pottery, gold and jewelled bracelets and necklaces, a gold sheathed dagger and, most important from the military angle, what is called the "Standard of Ur".

This standard is a slab of wood, eight inches by nineteen, covered with a mosaic of shells and coloured stones, which shows what is perhaps the earliest organised army in history. One side of the tablet shows a battle, the other the banquet celebrating the victory. The scenes are depicted in three strips on each side. On the first the king is receiving prisoners, while his chariot is held by his charioteer. The second strip shows the infantry, wearing helmets and carrying short, heavy spears. In the third strip, we see four war-chariots in action. They are high in front and open at the rear. The solid wheels probably had leather tyres. They are harnessed to asses, and each chariot has a crew of two—driver and spearman. There is a rack for spare spears.

The victory feast on the other side of the standard shows the king supping with six generals. They are seated, and servants bring the food, while soldiers parade the spoils of war and a bound prisoner. From the pictures, we can discern the nature of the army of Ur at that time, divided into light infantry, heavy infantry and the chariots.

EGYPT, ASSYRIA AND PERSIA

Lord Byron's poem, *Destruction of Sennacherib*, gives an imaginative picture of the warriors of long ago:

> The Assyrian came down like a wolf on the fold,
> And his cohorts were gleaming in purple and gold,
> And the sheen of their spears was like stars on the sea,
> When the blue wave rolls nightly on deep Galilee.

1. Warriors of the Stone Age, armed with bows and arrows, were painted by early artists on the walls of caves.

2. Sumerian soldiers depicted on the Standard of Ur (3000—2500 B. C.). Infantry and also charioteers are shown.

Three great civilisations followed the Sumerians, and they were all warlike. They were the Egyptians, the Assyrians and the Persians, and they overlapped each other during the period from 2000 to 600 B.C.

All three are mentioned in the Old Testament, and we can reconstruct much of their way of life from objects found in tombs, from temples, from paintings on tomb and temple walls, and sometimes from written records.

The tombs and temples of ancient Egypt have yielded the greatest amount of evidence, especially the tomb of Tut-ankh-amen, *circa* 1350 B.C. The tomb was packed with treasures buried with the king.

The Egyptians used axes, spears and swords, first of bronze and later iron. They also used bows and arrows and had very fine daggers. Officers wore light armour of linen reinforced with metal, or sometimes crocodile skin. Their helmets were often plumed. The ordinary soldier had only a shield for protection. Egyptian chariots were light and broad, and came into use about 1800 B.C. The iron wheels had spokes, an advance on the solid wheels. Egyptians had no cavalry. The charioteers were a small select corps; the majority of the army were foot soldiers, mainly bowmen.

The Assyrians, the heroes of Lord Byron's poem, flourished about 1000 B.C., and became the greatest military power of their day. They were the first to use cavalry, and their bowmen were famous for their skill. The Assyrian chariots were heavier than those of the Egyptians.

The Persians, who are called the Medes and Persians in the Old Testament, reached the peak of their power under Cyrus the Great, about 550 B.C. The core of the Persian army was the Immortals, a picked force of some 10,000 highly privileged men which provided the royal bodyguard. The remainder of the Persian army was provided by conquered peoples, unwilling soldiers who had to be driven into battle by the whips of their officers. Persian chariots sometimes had scythe blades fitted to the axles.

3. Pharaoh Rameses II, in the light Egyptian war-chariot, leads his troops into battle.

COLOUR PLATES

TOP LEFT: Figure of a Persian archer, from a frieze representing the King's Royal Guard.

TOP RIGHT: Detail of a mosaic, showing the battle between Alexander the Great and Darius at Issus.

BOTTOM: Carving of a Persian chariot from Persepolis (521—486 B.C.).

TOP LEFT: Arms and armour carried by a
Roman centurion.

ABOVE: Norman cavalry, from the world-
famous Bayeux Tapestry.

BOTTOM LEFT: Shield, helmet and sword of
a Roman soldier.

BELOW: Battle between the Anglo-Saxons and
the Normans at Hastings, in 1066, also from
the Bayeux Tapestry.

ABOVE: Guidoriccio da Fogliano, a prominent condottiere of the early 14th Century, from a fresco by Simone Martini.

LEFT: A 16th Century battle scene, from a manuscript bearing the title of Memoires de Philippe de Commines.

THE GREEKS

The Persian military power was finally overthrown by the Greeks, who succeeded them as first power in the old world until they, in turn, gave place to the Romans. Homer's *Iliad*, written about 700 B.C., is full of stories of the Greek soldiers at the siege of Troy, but it deals more with the legendary heroes, Achilles, Agamemnon and Hector, than the men they commanded. In the *Iliad*, the infantry fights in the Greek phalanx formation, a compact formation in close lines about sixteen abreast. The phalanx was the Greek infantry formation for centuries.

In the great days of ancient Greece, the army was well-organised and equipped. The infantry was armed with the sarissa, a long and heavy thrusting spear. The different ranks in the phalanx carried spears of varying lengths, up to seventeen feet. The phalanx was formed by the hoplites, conscripted from men who did not maintain horses but could afford to equip themselves with armour—breast-plate, greaves and helmets, small round shields, and sword and spear. Wealthier citizens could be called up with their horses to provide the cavalry, and poorer conscripts served as lightly-armed infantry.

When Alexander the Great set out to conquer the world in 336 B.C., the core of his army was a force of three thousand hoplites forming the phalanx, some six thousand light infantry in support, with, as the corps d'élite, several hundred cavalry. Alexander also had troops provided by his allies and a number of hired mercenaries. In India, Alexander met a new military force, the two hundred fighting elephants of King Porus. Alexander never used elephants himself, but they were used by later Greek commanders.

4. A soldier of a highly warlike race — the Hittites — who established an empire in Anatolia and reached the peak of their power in 1300 B. C.

5. Four Assyrians in full battle array share a chariot (c. 700 B.C.).

6. This fight between Greek soldiers of rival States appears on an amphora found at Vulci (c. 540 B. C.).

THE ROMAN ARMY

The Roman army, which conquered and ruled the civilised world of its day, was unequalled for morale, organisation and efficiency. Proudest of all was the Praetorian Guard, a select force of picked men who were the emperor's personal bodyguard—like the Persian Immortals, King Harold's Housecarles who died with him at Hastings, Napoleon's Imperial Guard, and the British Household Cavalry and Foot Guards of today.

The main first-line troops were the legions. There were, at different times, between twenty-five and thirty-five legions, each of about five thousand men. The invasion of Britain in A.D. 49 was carried out by four legions, the II, IX, XIV and XX, which with auxiliary cavalry and infantry

8

9

10

totalled about forty thousand men. The organisation of a legion was:

A legion	=	10 cohorts	of 480 men each
A cohort	=	6 centuries	of 80 men each
A century	=	10 contubernia	of 8 men each

A contubernium was the smallest unit in the army, like the modern infantry section. The eight men shared a tent and a pack-horse to carry it, and in barracks they shared a pair of rooms. Originally a contubernium was ten men, which would give a hundred for the century, six hundred for the cohort and six thousand for the full legion.

The legion was commanded by a legatus, with six staff officers and the camp prefect. The centuries were commanded by centurions, under the chief centurion who himself commanded the 1st Century. Next to the centurion was the aquilifer, the standard bearer who carried the silver eagle, the sacred symbol of the legion, which can be compared with the colours carried by European infantry in the seventeenth, eighteenth and nineteenth centuries. Below these were the other officers, in a carefully graduated series of ranks.

Each legion had a squadron of 120 mounted men, used as dispatch riders and scouts, and the first cohort had all the clerks, armourers and technicians of the legion's headquarters on its staff.

The auxilia, raised from the men of conquered provinces, was used as light infantry to screen the legions, operating in advance and on the flanks of the more heavily armoured imperial troops. The auxilia consisted of cavalry, infantry and mounted infantry. The cavalry (or alae, wings) was in regiments divided into sixteen troops of thirty-two men, making a total for the regiment of 512. The infantry was organised into cohorts and centuries, and the establishment of the mounted infantry, or *equitatae*, was 380 infantry and 120 cavalry, divided into centuries and troops.

The Roman foot soldier had two weapons, the sword, *gladius*, and the javelin, *pilum*. The sword was short, two feet long, with a broad double-edged blade. The scabbard was of wood or leather with bronze fittings, and it was sometimes gilded. In battle the javelin was hurled first, then the sword was drawn. The javelin was seven feet long, including the two-foot long iron head, and it could kill at a range of thirty yards. The sharp point could stick in a shield, which would then be pulled down by the weight; consequently the enemy often threw away the loaded shields as the legions advanced. The butt of the javelin was encased in metal, so that it could be thrust into the ground for defence against enemy cavalry.

The helmets were of bronze or iron, with hinged cheekpieces to protect the sides of the head, and a ridge to protect the eyes and nose; the back was swept down as protection for the neck. The legionaries wore plates of armour on back and chest, with flexible metal plates on the shoulders and front. There was also armour made of interlocking rings, or small "scales", sewn to the tunic in overlapping rows. The shield was leather or wood, bound with metal strips at the edges. It was rectangular and curved to cover the body, and it had a leather handgrip inside to be held over the forearm, and another so that it could be hung from the shoulder on the march. The soldier, who wore a woollen tunic to the knees and a linen undergarment beneath, had a thick woollen cloak for bad weather.

The Roman army conquered much of the then-known world, and was invincible for six centuries. Organised for every detail of service, strictly disciplined and superbly self-confident, the army of Rome surpassed any which had gone before, and was not to be equalled for a thousand years.

7. An Etruscan warrior (late 5th Century B. C.), whose people ruled Italy before the Romans.

8. Roman soldiers protecting themselves with shields while scaling a city wall.

9. Barbarians attacking a Roman fort. Plaster-cast from Trajan's column (113 A. D.).

10. Two Tetrarchs, warrior kings of the late Roman Period, on the front of St Mark's, the great cathedral of Venice.

11. Shinshongojin, a temple guardian of Japan (800 A. D.).

11

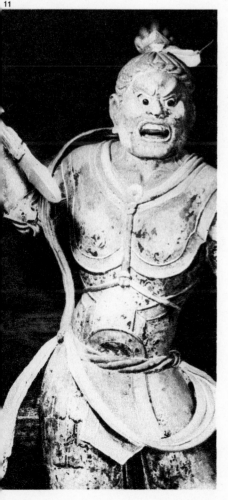

KNIGHTS AND MEN-AT-ARMS

12. Fierce and bloody attack by the Vikings on the shores of Britain (c. 900 A D.).

13. Impression of Attila the Hun (c. 450 A. D.).

14. Bronze statue of the great Charlemagne (742—814 A. D.).

15. Drawing of Saxons at the Battle of Hastings.

16. Ghengis-Khan (1162—1227), chief of the Mongol hordes.

When the Roman Empire collapsed in the fifth century A.D., European civilisation disintegrated. The Pax Romana had been maintained by force of arms, and when the authority of the Roman legions had gone, disorder quickly followed. The armies which warred across Europe in the Dark Ages had none of the efficient organisation of the Romans, and no central and unifying government. They depended on the prowess and genius of their commanders: Attila the Hun, in the last dying years of Rome; Charlemagne, King of the Franks and Emperor of the West, in the eighth century; and the Mongol overlord Genghis Khan, who conquered most of central Asia at the beginning of the thirteenth century, and whose son devastated eastern Europe. These and a host of other conquerors created new boundaries and new nations, and from them a new Europe emerged.

The armies which forged the new Europe used the network of splendid Roman roads, and fought mainly on horseback. Attila led a host of mounted archers, the Germans fought with heavily-armed cavalry, eastern armies rode small horses with consummate skill and, later in the period, knights and men-at-arms fought on gaily caparisoned war-horses. Only the English fought entirely on foot, even in their last great battle at Hastings against the Norman cavalry. Weapons did not change: the bow and arrow; the sword, sometimes heavy and two-edged, sometimes light and curved; the battle-axe; the spear, and the throwing javelin.

ANGLO-SAXONS AND VIKINGS

Britain provides an excellent example of the processes which created Europe through the five or six centuries after the fall of Rome. When the legions left Britain in 410 A.D., her unguarded coast was attacked and invaded by the Angles, Jutes and Saxons, heathen and very warlike Germanic peoples. The British, accustomed for nearly four centuries to the protection of the Roman army, were driven in large numbers further and further west, to take refuge in Cornwall and the mountains of Wales. England, taking its name from the Angles who settled there, was split into a number of small Saxon kingdoms.

In the ninth century came another invader, the fierce Vikings from Scandinavia. These sea-warriors—Danes and Norsemen—came in their beautifully built ships, high at stem and stern with a deep-swept gunwale, raiding the east coast of Britain and the west coasts of France and Spain, and sailing north and west to be the first to cross the Atlantic to America. At first they were content to raid the east coast of England, burning and looting, but soon they began to settle in East Anglia, spreading inland until they occupied more than half the land.

14

15

16

It was Alfred the Great, the Christian king of Wessex, who brought the Vikings to terms. At Ethandune, in 878, Alfred defeated the Danes, converted their leader, Guthrum, to Christianity and brought peace. The Danes occupied the east and north, and the Saxons the west and south of England. Soon the races mingled, and their blood was fused together to form a fresh race. This was the process which formed the new Europe, as the conquest of warriors created new nations.

ENGLISH VERSUS NORMAN

We have a wonderfully detailed picture of the soldier of the eleventh century in the Bayeux Tapestry. This is an enormous "strip cartoon", 231 feet long and 20 inches deep, which is preserved at Bayeux, in Normandy. In a series of seventy-two scenes embroidered on linen soon after 1066, it tells the story of King Harold of England and Duke William of Normandy, from Harold's visit to William in 1064, to William's victory over Harold at Hastings in 1066. The tapestry is in excellent condition and shows us countless details of warfare nine hundred years ago.

The Anglo-Saxon army was founded on the fyrd, called the landwehr in Europe. As reorganised by Alfred the Great and later by Canute, it imposed a double duty on all owners of five hides of land (about five hundred acres). For every five hides the owner had to provide one man, fully armed and equipped, to serve the king when required, and the owner himself had to report as well, also fully armed. In addition to the amateur soldiers of the fyrd, Harold had a force of from three to six thousand professional Danish soldiers, known as House-carles. In the battle the House-carles took the centre of the line, with the less experienced fyrd on the flanks.

The fyrd were organised in county "battalions" and formed up for battle in large wedges, with two or three men in the front, the wedge gradually

17. Bronze of a 7th Century soldier.

18. Byzantine fresco, depicting the arrest of Christ by soldiers wearing IIth Century armour.

19. Castle built by Crusaders at Krak, in Syria.

20. Engraving of the tomb of William Marshal in the Temple Church, London, as it was prior to damage by enemy action during the London blitz. It has since been restored.

21. Miniature from 'The Chronicles of St Denis', a French 14th Century manuscript showing Crusaders and their Saracen foes.

widening out behind them. The officers and the best fighters were in front of the close mass, the less experienced in the rear. The English weapons were spear, sword and, the favourite, battle-axe. Most of the fyrd only carried a shield for personal protection. The House-carles, and those of the fyrd who could afford it, wore a shirt of chain-mail, and a conical helmet with a bar to protect the nose. They were armed with a sword, five missile darts or javelins, and a heavy battle-axe. They carried large shields, pointed at the bottom, which they locked together as they awaited the enemy in line, thus making a formidable shield-wall. On the morning of the 14th October, 1066, King Harold took the centre of the line, in the midst of his House-carles, with the battalions of the fyrd on each flank, on Senlac Hill. He stood across William's road to London, awaiting his attack to decide the fate of England.

William of Normandy had destroyed his boats when he landed in Pevensey Bay, for he did not mean to return. He had drawn his army from far and wide, inviting well-equipped knights to join his expedition with their men, on the promise of grants of land in England. His army was mainly composed of cavalry, well-armed mounted knights and men-at-arms, supported by archers. The favourite Norman weapons were the heavy double-edged sword, the hurling javelin, and the arrows of the archers.

The Battle of Hastings was cavalry against infantry, the sword against the battle-axe. It lasted throughout the day, from early morning to dusk, and victory came for the battle-weary Normans only when King Harold fell, first to a chance arrow in the eye, then to a slashing sword cut from a mounted Norman knight. Harold died among the remnant of his House-carles, under his standards of the Dragon of Wessex and the Fighting Man. It was the last successful invasion of Britain, and the course of English history was changed with the dawn of a new era.

THE CRUSADES

The main military activity in the late eleventh and twelfth centuries was the crusades, campaigns undertaken by Christian nations to liberate Jerusalem and the Holy Land from the Moslem Turks. The developing knightly classes, with their elaborate rules of chivalry, saw in the crusades a chance to exercise piety with adventure and, probably, a chance for loot as well. It was fashionable as well as creditable to don the white surcoat with the cross over one's armour, and ride off to the Holy Land.

The First Crusade began at Constantinople in 1096, where the various contingents converged. Godfrey de Bouillon commanded an army of some 300,000, with which he invaded the Holy Land, captured Jerusalem and set up a Christian kingdom with himself as monarch. Other crusading barons took parts of the Holy Land for themselves and built strong castles to hold it. These stout crusader castles are still to be seen in Palestine and Syria.

The Holy Land did not, however, remain a peaceful Christian land, for a whole series of crusades followed. The Third Crusade, of 1190, had German, French and English contingents. The German army was commanded by Frederick I, Philip Augustus led the French, and Richard Coeur-de-Lion captained the English. The three armies converged on the great fortress of Acre, held by Saladin, the Sultan of Egypt, who was leading the Moslem world to drive the Christians from Palestine.

Little was achieved. Frederick was drowned on the way, and the French and English kings quarrelled. There was some stalwart fighting which produced many legends and, on the way back, Richard was captured and held as hostage in a German castle.

Pope Innocent III organised the Fourth Crusade, which started from Venice. But the crusaders changed their route and sacked Constantinople, the headquarters of Christianity in eastern Europe, instead of the Holy Land. In 1212 came the tragic Children's Crusade, in which 50,000 French and German children perished, or were taken as slaves by the Arabs. Other crusades followed but, by the end of the thirteenth century, the crusading spirit died out.

The crusades did not achieve their purpose of permanently liberating the Holy Land, but they had incidental value. When warlike barons and knights were away on a long-distance operation, they could not make war on each other at home, which meant peace for the common people. New forms of strategy and tactics were developed, and experience was gained in mounting large, long-distance expeditions. They also fostered the skill and the cult of knightly service.

During this period, armour developed, and the skill of the armourers became such that eventually the knight and his horse were encased in shining, beautifully-fashioned steel. Tournaments provided glittering spectacles in which fully-armoured knights, surcoats and shields ablaze with heraldic colours, fought with lance and sword, and demonstrated the art and science of skill at arms.

22. The longbowman and crossbowman of the 14th Century. The longbow played a major part in many English victories.

THE ENGLISH LONGBOW

The bow and arrow was the weapon of the earliest soldiers of whom we have knowledge, and it remained an important weapon up to the sixteenth century. In the Middle Ages, the crossbow was used, a mechanically-operated bow which shot iron bolts.

An important event occurred in England in the thirteenth century,

PLAYER'S CIGARETTES

19TH REGIMENT OF FOOT
Grenadier's cap, 1750.

PLAYER'S CIGARETTES

15TH (THE KING'S) LIGHT DRAGOONS;
Officer's full dress helmet, 1768.

PLAYER'S CIGARETTES

GRENADIER'S CAP,
1768-96

PLAYER'S CIGARETTES

LIFE GUARDS
Officer's full dress helmet, 1815.

PLAYER'S CIGARETTES

17TH LANCERS;
Officer's full dress cap, 1820.

PLAYER'S CIGARETTES

2ND DRAGOON GUARDS;
Officer's full dress helmet, 1820-34.

PLAYER'S CIGARETTES

15TH THE KING'S HUSSARS;
Officer's full dress shako, 1834.

PLAYER'S CIGARETTES

4TH (ROYAL IRISH) DRAGOON GUARDS;
Officer's full dress helmet, 1834-43.

PLAYER'S CIGARETTES

6TH DRAGOON GUARDS;
Officer's full dress helmet, 1855-71.

PLAYER'S CIGARETTES

12TH LANCERS;
Officer's full dress cap, 1859-81.

PLAYER'S CIGARETTES

15TH THE KING'S HUSSARS;
Officer's full dress busby, 1861.

PLAYER'S CIGARETTES

60TH RIFLES
(THE KING'S ROYAL RIFLE CORPS)
Officer's full dress busby, 1873(?).

23. At the battle of Poitiers, in 1356, the bow-men and knights of England overcame the flower of French chivalry.

when King Edward I, campaigning in Wales, noticed the power and accuracy of the Welsh archers using the longbow. Immediately, Edward I saw to it that the longbow became the principal weapon of the English soldier.

Soon a longbow stood in the chimney corner of every house and cottage in the land, and regular practice at the local butts became compulsory for all men. Young boys practised with bows of their own height, being promoted to larger ones as they grew, until they were able to use a man-sized bow. Six feet in length, and carefully made of selected, seasoned wood, this powerful weapon shot an arrow a yard long. In expert hands the arrow from a longbow could pierce plate armour at two hundred and fifty yards' range. It was the English bowmen of Edward III and Henry V who won the victories of Crécy, Poitiers and Agincourt, tumbling the hosts of the finely-armoured French cavalry to ruin.

A MEDIEVAL ARMY

The French chronicler Froissart supplied innumerable descriptions of medieval warfare and battle. Part of his account of the expedition of Edward III to France in 1359 shows how elaborately an army was equipped, and what attention was paid to the comfort and pleasure of the commanders. The army's baggage train, wrote Froissart, was more than six miles long, and the divisions of the army were so richly bedecked that "it was a joy to see them.

"The king of England and the great men of his host had ever with them, in their carriages, tents, pavilions, mills, ovens, and forges,to scythe and to bake and to forge shoes for horses; and for other things necessary. They had with them six thousand carts, each with at least four good horses brought out of England.

"They also took in the carts special leather boats, subtly wrought, and

COLOUR PLATES

TOP LEFT: The Battle of Culloden, in 1746, showing the Duke of Cumberland—known as 'The Butcher'.

BOTTOM LEFT: The Retreat from Moscow, in 1812, by Napoleon's army.

sufficient every one of them to take three men to cross rivers, and for fishing from, which gave the great lords much pleasure in Lent.

"Also the king had thirty falconers on horseback, with hawks, and sixty couple of hounds and as many greyhounds, so that nearly every day they hunted or hawked, and divers other great lords had hounds and hawks as well as the king.

"And whenever the host moved they went in three battles and each had a vanward (vanguard) and each lodged by itself, a league from the other."

This was an army of the fourteenth century, an army of nobles and knights in elaborate armour, with squires and richly-emblazoned banners, and men-at-arms, and always the redoubtable archers with the devastating fire-power of their longbows.

24. Led by Queen Phillipa of England at the battle of Nevil's Cross (1346), the English troops defeated those of King David of Scotland and took him prisoner.

24

24

GUNS AND THE PROFESSIONAL SOLDIER

"Artillery" in one form or another was used from the earliest days. In *II Chronicles*, chapter 26, verse 15, we read that, in the Eighth Century B.C., Uzziah "made in Jerusalem engines, invented by cunning men, to be set upon the towers and bulwarks to shoot arrows and great stones". The Romans used the *ballista*, a giant catapult. It is always a good idea to hit the other man while remaining out of his reach yourself, which is the principle of the arrow, the throwing javelin, and the sling-stone with which David slew Goliath. But a more lethal weapon was put in the hands of soldiers when gunpowder and the gun were invented.

CANNON

The English monk and philosopher Roger Bacon described the manufacture of gunpowder in 1248, and a German monk, Berthold Schwarz, invented the gun some time before 1330. The first guns were crude, unreliable and not without peril to the gunner. They were iron tubes with a touch-hole to which a burning match was applied. The earliest known siege gun was used in Italy in 1331, and some primitive kind of field gun was used by Edward III at Crécy, in 1346. In the Hussite Wars of 1419–1424, the religious conflict in Bohemia, light cannons were mounted on carts, a very early use of mobile field artillery. Similar field artillery was used in the Wars of the Roses for, in 1459, the Lancastrians accused the Yorkists of cheating by using "cartes with gonnes set before their bastilles".

There were many varieties of early cannon, from gigantic "bombards", which nowadays we should call mortars, firing enormous stone cannon-balls to batter down the walls of besieged castles or cities, to slender tubes firing thick arrows, sometimes burning. The development of the cannon was a slow business, for many problems of construction had to be overcome, but by the sixteenth century artillery was in general use in war on

25. The trebuchet, one of many siege-weapons.

26. Three devices used to break down city walls and gates.

27. An early hand-gun of the 15th Century.

28

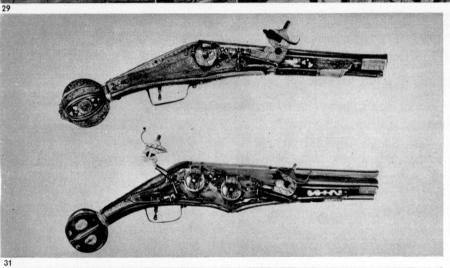

29

30

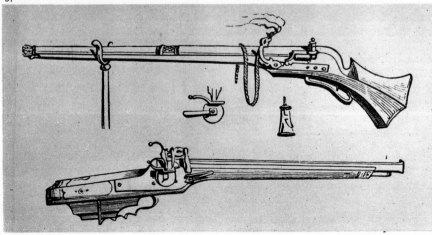

31

32

land and sea. Soldiers were proud of their big guns, and often gave them names. When Henry VIII besieged Tournay, in 1513, he named his twelve big guns after the apostles. St John got stuck in the mud.

HARQUEBUS AND MUSKET

The "handgun", the ancestor of the musket and the rifle, got off to a better start as there were less serious constructional problems. The first type was the matchlock, or harquebus, supported on a tripod for firing. It was a simple iron tube, down which powder and ball were rammed, with a touch-hole, at first on the top of the barrel and later on the side. A lighted "match" was applied to the touch-hole and the harquebus fired.

The first improvement was the "wheel-lock", which came into use in the early sixteenth century, and did away with the inconvenience of using a burning or glowing "match". The cock was armed with pyrites which, when lowered, pressed against the ribbed edge of a wheel projecting through the bottom of the priming pan. When the trigger was pulled, the wheel revolved and struck sparks from the pyrites, which fired the powder in the priming pan.

In the seventeenth century, the "flint-lock" musket brought better accuracy and speed of firing. When the trigger was pulled, a piece of flint, held in steel claws, fell and struck a piece of steel, throwing sparks into the priming pan, and so lighting the powder pressed behind the ball and its wad in the barrel. The flint-lock was the main weapon of infantry for two centuries, and the most famous musket of all—the British "Brown Bess"—was used, with minor modification, from Marlborough's wars of 1702–1709 through the whole of the eighteenth century to the battle of Waterloo, in 1815. Brown Bess was beautifully made, and deadly in the hands of the highly-trained British infantry. It has been said that Brown Bess won the British Empire.

EARLY PISTOLS

Pistols were developed alongside muskets, and were mainly used by cavalry. In the Thirty Years War of 1618–1648, the heavy German cavalry, the *reiters*, used pistols to great effect. They developed a special mode of attack, advancing in deep formation at the walk until the front rank charged, each man firing two pistols at point-blank range, then cleverly wheeling away to right and left in the caracole, and trotting to the rear to reload. Meanwhile, the second rank repeated the manoeuvre, and then the third, fourth and so on, until the original front rank was in position again. Thus a constant close-range fire was kept up until the enemy broke.

The British heavy dragoons of the late seventeenth century used pistols in a different way. Each dragoon expected to account for five of the enemy. The line charged and, at close range, every trooper fired a pair of pistols; then he hurled the heavy weapons at the heads of two more of the enemy, and finally drew his sword to account for the fifth.

The loading and priming of a musket was a complicated business, sometimes requiring a hundred precise drill-movements. The main ones were charging with powder, ball and wad and ramming home, and putting powder in the priming pan. Pikemen still had their place in the ranks, mingled with the musketeers to protect them during the process of reloading, and to attack the enemy "at push of pike", until bayonets were provided to fix on the barrels of the muskets.

28. Manuscript of the 15th Century, showing an assault on a castle.

29. Wheel-lock pistols made in Nuremberg (c. 1580).

30. An early form of siege-cannon employed in the 15th Century.

31. Two forms of arquebus used during the 16th Century.

32. Scottish Dragoon, in 1680.

ARMOUR AND BULLETS

The increasing efficiency of "hand guns" in the sixteenth century gradually gained the upper hand over personal armour. A bullet would drive chain mail into the body and cause a serious wound. Plate armour provided some protection for a while, but eventually that too had to give way to the power of the bullet. English statutes of 1672 and 1673 ordered cavalry to wear only the cuirass (breastplate and backpiece) and "pot-helmet", and to carry sword and pistols. The Duke of Marlborough, however, only permitted a breastplate to his men, as he did not consider it necessary to protect the back of good soldiers. So the bullet defeated the complete suits of personal armour, although the breastplate and backpiece are still worn in ceremonial dress by the British Household Cavalry.

The art and skill of the armourer were not lost, however, with the coming of firearms, for although armour was not worn for war after the beginning of the sixteenth century, it was still worn for tilting. Personal armour reached its greatest beauty in the early sixteenth century, especially inspired by three monarchs who shared the taste for chivalry and splendour: the Emperor Maximilian, King Francis I of France, and King Henry VIII of England. Examples of tilting armour of this period still exist, wonderfully fashioned, and splendidly chased and decorated. Armour was still worn throughout the sixteenth century and into the seventeenth. King Charles I had small suits of armour made for his two little sons at the outbreak of the Civil War, in 1642.

The study of armour is complicated and highly technical. Different nations had different styles, and details were always changing.

PROFESSIONAL SOLDIERS

In the middle of the thirteenth century a new kind of soldier came into being, the professional who "lived by the sword". Companies of well-equipped and highly-trained soldiers, with much esprit-de-corps, were available for hire by anyone who could pay them their price. The better they were, and the more successes they had achieved, the higher the price.

An early form of these professional soldiers were the condottieri, skilled commanders who had their own companies and who fought, for hire, for the rich Italian city-states in the thirteenth and fourteenth centuries. The condottieri were of every nationality and they had no interest at all in the cause of the wars they fought. They would change sides with no compunction if they were offered a higher fee. They were essentially professional soldiers—war was their trade.

Montreal d'Albarno, of Provence in southern France, was the first of the condottieri to give his private army a definite form, with strict discipline and elaborate organisation, and with barbaric licence towards civilians. The Grand Company, as it was called, grew to number 7,000 cavalry and 1,500 infantry, picked men who owed allegiance only to their commander. The fame, success and profit of a company depended entirely on the character and reputation of the commander, who was the proprietor.

The White Company, famous between 1360 and 1390, was commanded by the gallant Sir John Hawkwood, and consisted mainly of Englishmen. The White Company was used by Sir Arthur Conan Doyle as the background for his novel of that name.

The condottieri were succeeded as famous mercenaries by Swiss infantry. In the war between Switzerland and Burgundy of 1476–77, the Swiss

33. Man-at-arms in plate armour mounted on a Barden horse, accompanied by an archer equipped with bow, arrows and a leaden mallet (15th Century).

34. Henry VIII as he appeared in armour (16th Century).

35. Medieval jousting armour.

36. Pikemen in armour (17th Century).

37. Armour worn by James II.

37

soldiers were formed into massive squares in the tradition of the classical phalanx and, armed with long pikes, they overcame all their enemies, and maintained their superiority for fifty years. Their services were eagerly sought by other rulers who hired them for their campaigns. The Vatican still uses Swiss Guards, who wear the picturesque uniform of the days of their military glory.

After the Swiss came the German lansquenets, founded by the Emperor Maximilian (1459–1519). They were the best troops in Europe, and throughout the sixteenth and seventeenth centuries they were much in demand as mercenary troops. They fought with great distinction on the Protestant side in the Thirty Years War of 1618–1648. Military uniforms as we know them had not come into use; soldiers wore strange and extravagant versions of civilian clothes, but none more extravagant than the lansquenets. They were completely professional and, like other mercenaries, they fought for the employer who paid best. The French army of the sixteenth century was mainly composed of German lansquenets and Swiss troops.

It sometimes happened that both sides in a war had employed lansquenets, so that they met each other in battle. When this happened they fought brilliantly, but both sides were careful to cause no casualties. There were battles which lasted the whole day with no blood shed at all, surely the ideal kind of warfare. Mercenaries always preferred taking prisoners to killing, because of the ransoms.

As national armies came into being during the seventeenth century, the professional hired soldiers went out of business. They left an important tradition behind them, of professional skill, discipline, organisation and tactics, and of esprit-de-corps, which was taken up by the soldiers who succeeded them.

38. Highly bedecked Swiss mercenary. His fabulous uniform was designed to impress the enemy and boost his own morale.

39. German lansquenet of the 16th Century.

40. A mounted lansquenet.

41. Private soldier of Villiers Marines, 1702.

42. Russian cavalry officer (1817—1819).

NEW ARMIES
AND NEW
WEAPONS

Regular national standing armies came into being in the second half of the seventeenth century, and the modern soldier was bred in the many wars of the eighteenth and nineteenth centuries. The army became a profession, with central control and administration, and a hierarchy of command and ranks. With a permanent army it was only necessary in time of war to recruit additional men, who could speedily be drafted into units ot the existing army and trained by the regular officers and N.C.O.s.

With regular national armies came standard uniforms, with predominant colours for different countries: white for France and Austria, blue for Prussia, green for Russia and red for Britain. There were regimental variations within armies by using different facings—collars, cuffs and waistcoats. Regiments had different details of uniform as well, such as the arrangement of the buttons, still retained in the five regiments of British Foot Guards.

THE CAVALRY

The uniforms of the cavalry were always more lavish and colourful than those of the foot soldiers. The heavy cavalry was used for the powerful and massive charge to break the infantry line, while the light cavalry was used for skirmishing, escort duty and general support duties. Light cavalry were brilliant horsemen with a tradition of élan and high spirits. The first regiments of hussars were formed in the Imperial Austrian army at the beginning of the eighteenth century, and they quickly won a name as swift and fearless horsemen. Other nations followed suit and raised regiments of hussars. They all copied the uniform of the Austrian hussars, which was based on the Hungarian national costume of the seventeenth century, with a short cloak swinging from one shoulder.

Another type of light cavalry was the Lancers, which came into being towards the end of the eighteenth century, when the Austrians armed some of their cavalry regiments with lances, a weapon which had long been out of use. The first were the Uhlans, and the best were the Polish lancers, who served with the Austrian army. As with the hussars, lancers were quickly formed in other armies as well. The lancers, too, were highly decorative and wore distinctive helmets with a flat square top.

Dragoons were originally mounted infantry, using horses to get into position, then dismounting to fight as foot soldiers, but eventually they became part of the heavy cavalry. A typical feature of the cavalry officer's equipment was the sabretache, a square leather satchel hung on the left side by long straps from the belt, and usually magnificently decorated with regimental insignia. It also served to keep the sabre or sword in place, and prevented it from flopping when riding fast.

THE INFANTRY

The invention of the bayonet late in the seventeenth century put an end to the use of the pike. The first were "plug bayonets", pushed into the barrel of the musket to make it a pike. Then bayonets were fitted with a ring to fasten round the barrel, so that the musket could be fired while the bayonet was fixed. So the musketeer could charge with fixed bayonet, and the pikeman was no longer required, though sergeants continued to carry a half-pike as a mark of rank until the nineteenth century.

Two specialised types of foot soldier developed—the grenadiers and the light infantry, known as the "flank companies", because the one took post on the right and the other on the left of a battalion. Both the grenadiers and the "light-bobs" were picked for special qualities. The grenadiers' task was to advance close to the enemy and then hurl grenades; it called for strong nerves to light the fuse of the primitive grenades under fire, and then to stand up and hurl them when the fuse was well alight. Grenadiers wore tall mitre-like hats instead of hats with an obstructive brim.

The light infantry were picked for their marksmanship and keenness. They were the skirmishers and the scouts, and in the storming of a city the light infantry and the grenadiers formed the gallant "forlorn hope" or, as the French called them, the *enfants perdus*, the "lost boys". They led the storming parties and were the first to scale the walls.

Towards the end of the eighteenth century, the French formed regiments of grenadiers, and it was the gallantry of the British First Foot Guards against French grenadiers at Waterloo, in 1815, which won them the title of Grenadier Guards. The British army formed regiments of light infantry, and Sir John Moore collected together and trained a light infantry brigade at Shorncliffe camp in 1802. The British light infantry were trained as marksmen, taught to fight as individuals in open formation, and wore dark green uniforms with dulled buttons for camouflage. Their general briskness was reflected in the quicker march, and the light infantry regiments in the British army still march at 140 paces a minute instead of the usual 120.

THE ART OF FORTIFICATION

Fortification was developed to a fine art in the eighteenth and nineteenth centuries. The Romans had been masters of fortification, and of the assault as well, with their 150-foot mobile wooden towers, ballistae and other siege engines, and skilful mining. Strong walls, towers and moats and ditches had always been used, with corresponding techniques for overcoming them. But the great French Marshal Vauban, who died in 1707, set a new standard in the science of fortification. He devised well-nigh impregnable forts, star-shaped with bastions and demi-bastions, ravelins, traverses, scarpes and counter-scarpes and glacis. The intricate and scientific con-

43. Frederick the Great reviewing his troops.

44. Marlborough at the battle of Malplaquet.

45. Battle of Bunker Hill.

46. Washington crossing the Delaware.

47. The French retreat from Moscow.

48. Napoleon at Waterloo.

49. Wellington and Blücher at Waterloo.

50. Charge of the Light Brigade.

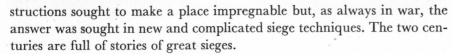

structions sought to make a place impregnable but, as always in war, the answer was sought in new and complicated siege techniques. The two centuries are full of stories of great sieges.

AN AGE OF GREAT GENERALS

With the profession of arms came great soldiers, men of outstanding ability and genius who, each in his way, made his own contribution to the art of war. France produced two in the seventeenth century —Turenne and Condé—both princes of royal blood, marshals of France and tutors of future generals of other nations who were proud to have served their apprenticeship under them. Turenne was a Dutch prince who began his military career at the age of fourteen under his uncle, Maurice of Nassau, and at nineteen entered the service of France, in which he was made colonel of an infantry regiment by Cardinal Richelieu. He served France with the greatest distinction, first under Louis XIII and then under the great Louis XIV. He was one of the great captains of the seventeenth century whose career Napoleon advised all soldiers to study.

The Prince of Condé began his military career in 1640 at the age of nineteen, campaigning in northern France, and from his first battle to his last, 1674, he showed outstanding military genius. With his colleague Turenne, he introduced new standards in generalship, strategy and organisation which were followed afterwards by generals of every nationality.

Another master of war was Frederick II—"The Great"—of Prussia. When he died in 1786, he left his country a splendidly-equipped regular army of 200,000 men, all trained in the most meticulous methods of drill. Britain produced two generals of outstanding skill—the Duke of Marlborough at the beginning of the eighteenth century, and the Duke of Wellington at the beginning of the nineteenth.

51. The 93rd Highlanders at Balaclava.

52. Field kitchen used in the Crimea (early war photograph).

53. American Civil War — standard of the 8th Pennsylvanian Regiment.

54. General Lee surrenders at Appomattox.

55. Union artillery in the Civil War.

56. A Zouave wounded at Chancellorsville in the service of the Unionists.

57. General Grant, the Union Army C.-in-C.

Marlborough's fame rests on his victories over France and her allies in the War of the Spanish Succession, at Blenheim (1704), Ramillies (1706), Oudenarde (1708) and Malplaquet (1709). Wellington's victories were won against the French of Napoleon in Spain between 1808 and 1814, and in Belgium at his greatest and final battle, Waterloo, in 1815. High among the great captains, perhaps highest, stands Napoleon himself, who fashioned from the revolutionary forces his *Grande Armée*, and by ruthless leadership and brilliant generalship dominated Europe for twenty years.

TWO CENTURIES OF WAR

The progress in the skills and organisation of soldiers and the emergence of great generals is the product of war, and the eighteenth and nineteenth centuries are important in the military art because they were filled with wars. Marlborough won his victories in the War of the Spanish Succession when, as usual, Britain and France were on opposite sides.

Frederick the Great fought a number of campaigns, the most important being the War of the Austrian Succession (1740–1748) and the Seven Years War (1756–1763). Most of Europe was involved in both these wars, with Britain and France on opposite sides. In the Seven Years War, Frederick was surrounded by enemies—Austria, France, Russia, Sweden and Saxony—with Britain his only ally. Frederick crowned his reputation as a great commander by his skill, and he was brilliantly served by the armies of Britain and Germany. One of the battles was Minden, fought on August 1st, 1759, when a brigade of five British regiments of foot won lasting glory by attacking and defeating an overwhelming number of French cavalry.

The Seven Years War was taken far afield by Britain and France. In 1757, Clive defeated the French and their Indian allies at Plassey, at one blow putting an end to French influence in India and laying the

foundations of the British Indian Empire. Two years later, Wolfe won Canada from the French by the victory of Quebec.

58. Prussian infantry charge French positions during the Franco-Prussian War (1870—1871).

THE AMERICAN WAR OF INDEPENDENCE

In two decades Britain won an empire in India and in Canada, and lost her North American colonies. Trouble between the colonists and the home government reached a head in 1775, which led to a war from which was born the United States of America. The dispute was originally over taxes. The colonists, with good reason, first resented and then refused to pay taxes to a British Government in which they had no representation. Incidents increased until the colonists began to arm themselves and the British garrison was ordered to put down the threatened insurrection.

The first skirmish between armed colonists and garrison troops was at Lexington in April, 1775, which was followed by a full-scale engagement in June at Bunker Hill. In the early days, the trained regular troops had little difficulty in overpowering the rebels, but the situation changed when the organisation and equipment of the colonists improved, and when they found a commander-in-chief of outstanding calibre in General George Washington, who became the first President of the United States. The British Government had to move in troops from the West Indies and from England, and what had at first seemed to be a minor insurrection became a full-scale war.

It was a strange kind of war to the British soldiers, trained and experienced in fighting in massed close formation. The colonists avoided such battles and were content to fight in the open, over the wide spaces of America. They were fine shots, used to hunting, or fighting Red Indians, and they fought as enterprising individuals rather than as disciplined units. It was a war of scouting, of advancing under cover, or skirmishing and

9. Scene at a Civil War military camp.

sharpshooting. Moreover, the British were used to fighting the French, which seemed natural; but they were uneasy at having to fight their own countrymen.

The colonists made their formal declaration of independence in 1776, after a lull in the fighting during the winter, and the campaign of intricate manoeuvre continued, while the British generals tried to corner the enemy and Washington cleverly kept the situation fluid. The British had successes, such as the Battles of Brooklyn and Brandywine, but neither were decisive. Then, in October, 1777, Washington won his first great success at Saratoga, where General Burgoyne's army of 5,700 was forced to surrender.

The war continued for three more years, although Britain was by no means unanimously behind the government. In 1780, Charleston, the capital of South Carolina, was taken by the British and a victory was won at Camden. The end came in 1781 with the capture of Yorktown by General Washington after a three-week siege, and shortly afterwards the British army in America surrendered. In 1782, Great Britain recognised the United States of America as an independent sovereign state.

THE NAPOLEONIC WARS

The emergence of Napoleon Bonaparte, an artillery officer in the army of the French Revolution, as First Consul of France and then as Emperor afflicted Europe with tremendous wars for twenty years. Napoleon's armies marched into Germany, Italy and Spain and, his great blunder, into Russia. Napoleon's genius, his ruthless subjection of everything to military might, and the superb self-confidence of his *Grande Armée*, put all Europe at his feet.

Napoleon suffered defeat in Russia because the enemy withdrew before him and left him at the mercy of the Russian winter, forcing him to make the grim retreat from Moscow. In Spain his armies faced the one enemy which was to bring about his ruin, the British army under Wellington.

Wellington inflicted and kept open a running sore in the side of Napoleon's great empire with a patient and brilliant campaign which lasted six years. Wellington constructed a strong base in the Lines of Torres Vedras, near Lisbon, from which he advanced each spring deeper and deeper into Spain. Between 1809 and 1814 he won a series of great victories which are emblazoned on the colours of every British regiment—Talavera, Busaco, Albuera, Badajoz, Salamanca and Vittoria—until the French were driven over the Pyrenees and back into France. Napoleon himself faced Wellington for the first time in 1815 at Waterloo. There, in a long and furious battle, in which the British were assisted towards the end of the day by a German army under Blücher, Napoleon was finally defeated, and he and his great empire fell.

THE CRIMEAN WAR

War returned to Europe in 1854, an unnecessary and sadly muddled war in the Crimea. Among the complicated causes was a dispute between Russia and Turkey over the custody of the Holy places in Jerusalem, and France and Britain allied themselves to Turkey against Russia. For the first time the ancient traditional enemies fought side by side, which was somewhat astonishing to the people of those days.

A combined British and French expeditionary force sailed to the Black Sea in 1854 and encamped at Varna, where cholera struck, the first of the many misfortunes which the British soldiers were to suffer. From Varna the allied force sailed to the Crimea, to invest the Russian Black Sea port of Sebastopol. As the invading forces marched inland, they were confronted by a strong Russian army strongly established on a ridge by the River Alma. Through the superb fighting of the British infantry the position was taken, the march proceeded, and a base was established near Sebastopol at the small port of Balaclava.

A Russian attempt to dislodge the British from Balaclava was foiled in October, 1854, by two historic cavalry actions. In the first the British Heavy Brigade charged and overcame a mass of Russian cavalry three times their number. On the same day the Light Brigade, mistaking their orders, charged the Russian guns down a narrow ravine, under murderous fire from front and both flanks.

Two weeks later the French and British infantry won glory at the Battle of Inkerman. A surprise attack was made by strong Russian forces, charging downhill in mist and drizzling rain. The Allied infantry stood their ground and fought them off. It was essentially a soldier's battle; direction and control from commanders was impossible, and the men fought where they stood, rallying when driven back, with units intermingled and confused. There was nothing at fault with the soldiers who fought in the Crimea, but there was a great deal wrong with the administration and organisation behind the lines.

Rations were unreliable, clothing was of poor quality and tragically insufficient for men serving in the trenches in the Russian winter, there was an insufficiency of tents and materials for building huts. Men froze to death in the trenches, epidemics and sickness took a fearful toll. It was the first time that newspaper reporters were officially permitted to be present at a war and, to the great displeasure of the authorities, Howard Russell of *The Times* sent home withering reports which opened the eyes of the public to the gross mismanagement. It was in the Crimea that Florence Nightingale did her gallant pioneer work in nursing, which was the beginning of a properly organised military nursing system.

The miserable war, touched with glory at the Alma, Inkerman and Balaclava, ended with the fall of Sebastopol in September, 1855, following a heavy bombardment and the masterly withdrawal of the Russian garrison to the northern part of the town.

THE AMERICAN CIVIL WAR

The Civil War which broke out in America in 1861 lasted four years, and ranged far and wide over the land. The immediate cause was the secession of eleven southern states from the Union, but basically it was fought on the question of slavery. In the north, slavery was abolished; in the south, slaves were used in the cotton fields and were a part of the way of life.

As always with civil wars, the conflict was passionate and ruthless; more than two thousand separate battles are recorded. The war was remarkable for the endurance, courage and persistence of both sides, and for the energy and brilliance of the commanders, among them General Robert E. Lee of the Southern (Confederate) States, and President Lincoln who directed the military policy of the Northern (Union) States.

The first engagement was at Charleston in April, 1861, where Fort Sumter, held by only seventy Union troops, was besieged and captured. Thereafter the war was waged mercilessly all over the country, with clever tactical marches and manoeuvres and countless bloody engagements and battles. The final battle was fought in April, 1865, at Five Forks, and this led to General Lee's surrender to General Grant. The Northern States were victorious, slavery was finally abolished throughout the land and,

TOP RIGHT: British troops capture a German occupied village in Flanders.

BOTTOM RIGHT: The death of Prince Albert the Kaiser's uncle, at the hands of Senegales during the Battle of Charleroi.

as resentment and soreness gradually died down, the United States emerged stronger and more united than before.

The American Civil War saw the first general use of the breech-loading rifle with the percussion cartridge. The machine-gun, in a primitive form, also came into use for the first time. The Gatling machine-gun was clumsy compared with later developments, but it fired a stream of bullets in rapid succession, and pointed the way to the weapon which was to revolutionise infantry tactics.

The Franco-Prussian War of 1870, which ended with the siege of Paris, also foreshadowed the deadliness of new weapons. The French used the *mitrailleuse*, which had thirty-seven rifle barrels revolving round the breech. Both French and Germans used new types of rifles and artillery.

THE SOUTH AFRICAN WAR

The war which can be called the last of the old kind was fought between Britain and the Boers in South Africa between 1899 and 1902. The Boers were the Dutch settlers, and they were fine shots and splendid horsemen. The traditional British red tunics made a man a dangerously clear target for such marksmen, so they were changed for the safer drab khaki.

The British used the new and very accurate Lee-Enfield rifle and, most important of all as a portent for the future, the Maxim machine-gun. This was entirely new, with a single water-cooled barrel firing bullets fed from a belt. The Maxim could fire between six and seven hundred rounds a minute. Another new feature was the balloon, and three Balloon Sections, R.E., served for observation and directing artillery fire. The Boers were 35,000 strong at the outbreak of the war, or twice the British number, and they were nearly all mounted. They used Männlicher and Mauser rifles and wore double ammunition bandoliers round their shoulders.

). A British soldier, dressed in the 'new' khaki, leaves for South Africa at the time of the Boer War.

1. Boer riflemen in action near Ladysmith.

2. Soldiers of a Boer commando encamped outside Ladysmith, Natal.

COLOUR PLATES

OP: This armoured personnel carrier typifies the mobility of present-day infantry.

OTTOM: An artist's concept of the Shillelagh surface-to-surface guided missile, now being developed for the U. S. Army.

The South African campaign covered great distances of open country, the rolling veldt. A feature was the long marching column, escorted by cavalry, and always vulnerable to sudden attack. There were many small engagements and a few large-scale battles. Fierce fighting often took place round rocky outcrops, where the attackers had room to manoeuvre in the veldt. There were also three famous sieges, when the Boers closed in on the towns of Kimberley, Ladysmith and Mafeking in the early weeks of the war. The stubborn resistence of the besieged, and the exploits of the columns marching great distances to their relief, are among the most memorable features of the war.

Ladysmith was invested by the Boers on November 2nd, 1899, and held out for 120 days. It contained 10,000 men under Sir George White, as well as a considerable civilian population. Rations were cut to the barest minimum, the horses and then the mules were slaughtered for food. Bread was poor and very scarce. It was very hot by day, and water was limited. Dysentery became rife.

Fortunately for the besieged, the Boers had little artillery, but they did have one six-inch gun which was called "Long Tom". Someone was always on watch with a telescope in Ladysmith and, when the flash was seen, a whistle was blown for everyone to take cover.

There was no thought of surrender in any of the besieged towns, but conditions were grave indeed in Ladysmith when, on February 28th, 1900, after 120 days of siege, a relieving column under General Buller reached them, dispersed the Boers and, led by the Guards, rode into the town triumphantly.

Mafeking, on the western border of the Transvaal, contained a small British force under Colonel Baden-Powell, which was besieged by the Boers. The town held out, suffering acute privations, until it was relieved after 217 days of siege.

At the start of the eighteenth century, Marlborough's armies fought in bright uniforms, in close formation, with muzzle-loading flint-locks and pikes. At the end of the South African War, soldiers wore khaki and fought with high-velocity bullets fired from rifles and machine-guns, and high-explosive shells from long-range guns. In Marlborough's time, an army was mustered in ten thousands; in the First World War, the dead were counted by the million.

MILITARY FORMATIONS

At this point in the history of the development of armies as we know them today, it would be helpful to consider how they are organised.

The size and precise make-up of military formations varies considerably from country to country, and in accordance with exact requirements at any particular time.

Naturally, the outbreak or threat of war necessitates expansion of forces, and the end of hostilities generally has the opposite effect.

However, taking British usage as an example, it is possible to give an outline of the general structure of an army and also an approximate idea of its chain of command.

Leaving aside the top governmental level of command—which has been reorganised in Britain with the Ministry of Defence co-ordinating the work of all three Services from Whitehall—we find that the Army is divided into a number of home and overseas Commands, each with its Commander-in-Chief.

53. British troops entrenched at Frayers Farm, Modder River, South Africa.

54. Introduction of the field-grey uniform to the German Army, in 1910.

55. Bulgarian soldier giving a drink to a wounded Turkish captive during the Balkan Wars.

This C.-in-C. is responsible for all the units and sub-units into which his Command is divided, for their efficiency, and for the well-being of every soldier in their ranks.

Starting with just such a soldier—an infantryman holding the lowest rank of all, Private—the pyramid of organisation is built up as follows. The Private's Section, led by a Lance-Corporal or Corporal (non-commissioned officer), is one of three making up a Platoon, commanded by a commissioned officer—Second-Lieutenant or Lieutenant—assisted by a Sergeant (N.C.O.). Three such platoons form a Company, commanded by a Major or Captain, assisted by a warrant officer with the rank of Company Sergeant-Major.

Six companies—possibly comprising four of rifles, and one each for support and headquarters, H. Q. being responsible for transport—might well make up the Battalion. The Commanding Officer (or C.O.) of this formation holds the rank of Lieutenant-Colonel, and many important duties in the battalion are undertaken by a warrant officer called the Regimental Sergeant-Major.

A Brigade usually consists of three battalions commanded by a Brigadier, and the formation above that is called a Division. This is likely to contain three infantry brigades, and also units of other arms of the service—such as gunners, engineers, signals—to make the formation largely self-sufficient. The officer in command is a Major-General.

The division, and any other divisions or lesser formations in the Command, are grouped together in charge of the Commander-in-Chief, possibly holding the rank of Lieutenant-General.

Higher still, the British Army has the ranks of General and Field-Marshal, awarded to officers appointed to special positions (such as Chief of the General Staff) and, in wartime, to those in charge of very large formations. Comprising several divisions, for instance, there is a Corps (perhaps commanded by a Lieutenant-General), and an Army (General).

The vast numbers engaged in the battles of twentieth century world wars have sometimes necessitated the introduction of a formation even larger than an army, and this is known as a Group of Armies. Those formed on the Russian Front during World War II contained as many as 2,000,000 men in 100 divisions.

Whilst divisions vary considerably in size, they are generally composed of from 11,000 to 15,000 men.

General Omar Bradley's Army Group of 2,500,000 men in the latter days of World War II was, however, made up of only 60-odd divisions, because it was United States policy to form unusually large divisions.

There are a considerable number of variations of size and name regarding smaller formations also, even if we take only the British Army as an example, and this applies particularly to units belonging to the various supporting Corps.

In the Royal Armoured Corps, which contains all the British cavalry regiments, the formation is as for mounted troops; a private is a Trooper, and working upwards the subdivisions are a troop, a squadron and a regiment. The Royal Engineers has Sappers instead of private soldiers, and the organisation is adjusted to suit the different engineering functions of a unit. Artillery is organised into troops and batteries of guns. The private is a Gunner and the corporal is a Bombardier.

The modifications are, in fact, legion, for any army has to adjust its organisation to the pressure of circumstances and necessity, but the broad structure and chain of command always remains much the same, with great similarities the world over.

THE FIRST
WORLD WAR

The war of 1914–1918, World War I, changed the nature of warfare; it was no longer solely the business of the professional soldiers, it became something new—total war. The vastness of the conflict and the immensity of the armies engaged brought every able-bodied man who could be spared from essential industry into uniform. The skill of the scientist produced deadlier weapons, casualties were on a scale never before imagined. The countries concerned were mobilised, both the fighting services and industry, entirely for the war effort; the one thought was for victory.

The new doctrine of total war was introduced by Germany. She first marshalled her people and economy for victory, and she then introduced new methods: poison gas in battle, the bombing of enemy countries, and the sinking of unarmed merchant ships by submarine attack.

WORLD WAR

Germany, Austria and Hungary, known as the Central Powers, declared war on Russia and France in August, 1914. The initial move had been the invasion of Serbia by Austria after the assassination in June of the Archduke Francis Ferdinand of Austria. The assassination was the event that released rivalries and tensions which had built up over a long period. Following the declaration of war, German troops marched into Belgium on August 3rd, and France went to the rescue of her small neighbour. Great Britain was pledged to help Belgium if she was attacked, so she declared war against Germany on August 4th.

Within hours, Canada, Australia and New Zealand, and then South Africa followed Great Britain's lead. Japan declared war on Germany, but fought mainly at sea; Italy joined the Allies in 1915, and the United States of America in 1917. Turkey entered the war on the side of the Central Powers, and the Balkan states were divided between the two warring groups.

The first phases of the war were Austria's invasion of Serbia, and the German moves westward against France and her allies, and eastwards against Russia. Later, however, the war spread—to the Dardanelles, Salonika, Mesopotamia and Arabia, and to East Africa. But it was on the Western Front, in France and Belgium, that the conflict was fiercest, and it was there, after four years of bitter warfare, that ultimate victory was won. Russia collapsed in 1917, and the campaigns in the other theatres were subsidiary to the main conflict.

Germany made her onslaught on France and Belgium with an army of a million men, plentifully supported by heavy guns. France was able to man her defences quickly with a force nearly as great, but Great Britain's regular army amounted to only 160,000 men for, being an island, she depended mainly on the Royal Navy, then the largest and most powerful in the world.

The British Expeditionary Force which went to France at the beginning of August, 1914 ,was, however, of the highest quality; it was perfectly equipped, brilliantly trained, and so accurate and fast in rifle firing that the Germans believed at first that they were equipped with machine-guns. The British Expeditionary Force was described as a "rapier among scythes". It was, of course, an entirely voluntary army, in contrast to the continental armies composed of men conscripted by law.

Britain's second line was her Territorial Army, a force of public-spirited men who gave up their weekends and their summer holidays to train as soldiers, and the territorial divisions soon followed the regular army to France. An appeal for volunteers met with such a good response that, by

66. Belgian troops prepare for action.

67. French soldiers even hurled lumps of rock to dislodge the Germans from hillside trenches.

68. British 'tommies' behind the lines in France.

69. German storm-troopers advancing across no-man's-land.

the end of August, 1914, more than a million civilians had left their jobs to become soldiers of the "New Army". By 1915, more than three million had volunteered. The new kind of war was so violent, however, and the casualties so enormous, that even more were needed; consequently, in 1916, for the first time in British history, conscription was introduced, and every able-bodied man who could be spared from industry was enlisted in the armed forces.

The war in France and Belgium was mobile for the first sixteen weeks. The large French and the small British and Belgian armies tried valiantly to stem the sweeping tide of the German Army as it flowed south down France towards Paris. The British Expeditionary Force fought a gallant rearguard action in the retreat from Mons, and the Allies stood at bay behind the River Marne on a line which centred on Verdun. Here was fought the Battle of the Marne in the second week of September, a desperate attempt to stop the German advance on Paris and the Channel ports. After four days' furious fighting, a sign of the ferocity of the battles to come, the Germans were thrown back beyond the River Marne, and Paris was saved. A new line was formed from the sea at Ostend southeast to Switzerland, with the British Expeditionary Force moved up to the left of the line around Ypres.

THE FIRST BATTLE OF YPRES

Both sides had the same plan, to break through the enemy's defences at Ypres, twenty miles from the coast near Dunkirk. The German plan was to break through and wheel left, to "fold up" the Allied line; the Allied

70. Canadian machine-gunners manning she holes on Passchendaele Ridge.

71. A typical French infantryman of the Firs World War.

72. 'Well, if you knows of a better 'ole, go t it!' (Bruce Bairnsfather's famous cartoon).

70

71

A map of the general position in Europe during World War I.

ALLIED POWERS
CENTRAL POWERS
CENTRAL POWERS
OCCUPIED TERRITORY
NEUTRAL COUNTRIES
← ATTACKS

plan was to break through and wheel right, to fold up the German line. The first Battle of Ypres began on the 19th October and lasted five weeks. The Germans attacked with the utmost violence, with heavy artillery and masses of infantry, in an attempt to break through and win a quick victory. The French and British armies fought with equal tenacity, their line becoming thinner as their casualties rose, determined to guard the Channel ports and Great Britain a few miles beyond.

The line held, through the superhuman endurance of the troops, and Paris, the Channel ports and Britain were saved. But the cost was appalling. For example, the 1st Battalion the Gloucestershire Regiment marched to Ypres with twenty-six officers and more than a thousand other ranks. Four weeks later they marched back with two officers and less than two hundred men. The terrible losses of the Gloucesters were by no means unique. The British Expeditionary Force, the highly trained and splendid army of 160,000 men, was virtually destroyed at Ypres. It had sacrificed itself by stopping the onslaught of the mighty German war machine. By its sacrifice it had saved Britain and, although it could not then be perceived, it had laid the foundations of the final victory over Germany.

TRENCH WARFARE

But that victory still lay four years ahead. After the Battle of Ypres, the two armies dug themselves in with defensive trench systems, protected by barbed wire, defended by machine-gun posts, and supported by massive artillery. Between the trenches was the hideous desolation of No-man's-land—a waste pitted with shell craters. In the winter, the trenches were often knee-deep in water and mud; raids were made across No-man's-land, swept by machine-gun fire. The men in the trenches were mercilessly mortared and shelled. All the colour, glitter and romance was drained from war, to be replaced by grim and sordid discomfort and death.

The expectancy of life of a junior officer in the trenches was three days. After ten days in the front line, troops marched back to their comfortless billets, utterly exhausted by their vigil, filthy, and often with nothing dry but their rifle-breeches and ammunition. Ten days' rest followed, and then —back to the front line, with raids, attacks over the top, and bullets, grenades, mortar bombs and shells. Steel helmets were issued as a protection against shrapnel.

A wry and gallant humour was bred in the British Army. A serious wound was called a "Blighty one", bad enough for the envied casualty to be sent home to "Blighty". Bruce Bairnsfather's cartoons show the grim humour of the men who refused to be cast down by the ghastly conditions.

Men joked as they went over the top into an inferno of shell-fire and machine-gun bullets, through a jungle of barbed wire, across the nightmare wilderness of craters and corpses. The songs they sang are memorials to that gallant and irrepressible spirit—*It's a Long Way to Tipperary, Little Grey Home in the West, Keep the Home Fires Burning,* and *Pack up your Troubles in your Old Kit Bag.*

The first rough trenches of the winter of 1914–15 were later improved with dug-outs, revetting, trench-boards, and an increasingly complicated system of support trenches. From time to time, attempts were made by both sides to straighten the line or to remove an enemy bulge, and battalions, brigades or divisions would scramble out of the trenches, with fixed bayonets and hand grenades ready, to advance through the hell of shells and bullets. Major attacks were mounted to try to break through the enemy's lines, but always the defences proved stronger than the offensive. The cost of the battles on the Western Front, and in the German-Russian battles on the Eastern Front, was appalling. To take but two examples, both from the Western Front: at the second Battle of Ypres, in April and May, 1915, the British casualties alone were 2,150 officers and 57,125 other ranks, of whom 10,125 were killed; and at the Battle of Loos, in September, 1915, the British losses in twenty-four days were 2,407 officers and 57,985 other ranks.

Trenches, barbed wire and machine-guns brought about deadlock. Germany tried to starve Britain into submission by submarine warfare, sinking the merchant ships on which her survival depended. In April, 1917, 196 ships with a total tonnage of 600,000 were torpedoed, but the Royal Navy eased that threat with the escorted convoy system. Another German attempt was the introduction of a particularly horrible new weapon, poison gas, which was first used at the second Battle of Ypres, in 1915, and later came to be used by both sides. But the issue of gas-masks and familiarity with the weapon blunted its edge, though increasingly terrible gases were employed.

The German air raids on Britain, first with Zeppelin airships and then with aeroplanes, introduced yet another horror to war, and brought civilian men, women and children into the firing line. The flying machine was developed, and fighter biplanes fought their private battles high in the air. Victory, however, was only to be won by the armies fighting on the ground, and in France and on the Eastern Front, men died in their tens of thousands for the gain or loss of a few yards of ground.

THE RUSSIAN FRONT

Germany, and her ally Austria-Hungary, began the war with a simple plan. They would destroy the French, Belgian and British armies in France in six weeks; then they would be able to use their whole strength against Russia, who would be defeated, they thought, before Christmas, 1914. It did not work out like that. The Allies were desperately hard-pressed in France, but their quickly-formed line held and, instead of being vanquished in six weeks, Germany herself was to be vanquished after four years. Germany was never able, therefore, to employ her whole power against Russia, and the war on the Eastern Front lasted three years.

Russia had vast resources of manpower which gave her a superiority in numbers of two to one over the Central Powers. But she was backward industrially, and Germany had the advantage in weapons and equipment, as well as much better roads, railways and communications. It was to the German advantage, therefore, to fight as close to their own frontiers as possible, instead of advancing into the inhospitable waste-lands of Poland and Russia.

The first Russian attack was made in August, 1914, when an army which far outnumbered the enemy invaded East Prussia. But brilliant generalship and superior mobility and arms gave the Germans a great victory at Tannenberg, at the cost of a quarter of a million Russian casualties.

The next Russian attack was made with an immense force, seven armies massed in a great phalanx. It seemed that such might must be invincible, and Russia's allies rejoiced at the certain success of the Russian "steamroller" which was to flatten all opposition on the road to Berlin. Again, however, German skill and mobility prevailed and the slow-moving giant was overcome by its smaller but nimbler opponent. The Germans attacked the junction between the armies, separated them and broke them,

73. A military patrol car operating in Petrograd (now Leningrad) during the fighting between rival revolutionary forces.

74. Revolutionist Boris Gregevitch aroused new patriotism in the Russian Army.

throwing the steam-roller completely out of gear. Gradually shortage of ammunition forced the Russians to fall back and, copying their allies on the Western Front, they dug a defensive line of trenches which they held during the winter of 1914–1915.

The greater space in the east made mobility possible as it never was in France, and great battles swayed back and forth throughout 1915 and 1916. The pattern was always the same: massive Russian armies, handicapped by an insufficiency of equipment and supplies, failing to overcome the smaller but better equipped German and Austrian armies. The Russian losses were tremendous and, gradually, the morale of her men suffered until, in the spring of 1917, revolution shook Russia from top to bottom. The Czar and his inefficient and corrupt government were swept away. After six months of political confusion, the Bolshevik Government was in full control, and signed an armistice with Germany in December, 1917.

Russia had lost more than a million men in battle, but her contribution to the Allied cause was incalculable. Throughout three desperate years she had kept large German and Austrian armies engaged while her allies fought for their lives in France.

THE BALKANS AND ITALY

The whole world-wide conflagration had been sparked off by a pistol fired in Serbia, in the town of Sarajevo, at the end of June, 1914. The shot murdered the Archduke Francis Ferdinand of Austria, and it was that deed which set the guns roaring for four dreadful years. The assassination brought a highly dangerous and complicated political situation in the

75

76

77

75. A field service held for Russian soldiers on the Polish front.

76. Women's battalions were raised to help in the overthrow of Russia's Czarist regime.

77. Arab prisoners being marched into Tripoli by Italian soldiers.

Balkans to a head; Austria attacked Serbia, and immediately Europe was plunged into war.

Serbia (now the southern part of Yugoslavia) fought most gallantly against her powerful foe, and with the Central Powers engaged in the west and east, she was able to drive the Austrian army which attacked her back to the Danube. But, in July, 1915, Bulgaria—Serbia's eastern neighbour—entered the war on the side of Germany and Austria-Hungary, and brought off the famous "stab in the back". Serbia was overrun and submerged.

Italy entered the war on the side of the Allies in May, 1915, and trench warfare like that in France developed between the Italian armies and those of Austria in the foothills of the Alps. Italy's part in the overall strategy was vitally important, because she engaged strong Austrian forces which could otherwise have joined the Germans in the west or east. This pressure against the Central Powers from the south was so important that British, French and, later, American armies joined the Italians.

As well as the trench warfare there was fighting in the mountains, which called for special skill in the manhandling of guns and equipment, and in existing in the harsh mountain conditions during winter. The Italians suffered a grievous defeat at Caporetto in October, 1917, but twelve months later they achieved the final defeat of the Austrian Army at the Battle of Vittorio Veneto.

THE DARDANELLES AND SALONIKA

In 1915 a daring plan was made to cripple Turkey, and so remove her threat against vital British and Allied interests in the eastern Mediterra-

78. Australian soldiers study enemy trench periscopes with interest.

79. An assault by Australian troops across Anzac Beach, Gallipoli.

80. Gurkhas manning a Lewis-gun emplacement on the Palestine front.

81. Tanks and infantry advancing during the capture of Grevillers by New Zealanders.

nean. A strong force, which contained Australian and New Zealand troops, sailed through the Mediterranean to force the narrow passage of the Dardanelles and capture Constantinople, now Istanbul. Its success would have had many advantages, among them the opening of a supply route to Russia.

The landing was made at Cape Helles on April 25th, 1915. The Australian and New Zealand troops—the Anzacs—and their comrades performed the impossible; they made a successful landing on narrow beaches thick with barbed wire and swept by machine-gun and artillery fire from the rugged hills which backed the beaches. The casualties were terrible, but the landing was made and the troops dug in; against tremendous odds, they held on. To hold on, however, was all that could be done—penetration proved to be impossible.

A second landing was made in July at Suvla Bay, a few miles to the north of the Anzac beaches, and once again it was only by the greatest gallantry and at a dreadful loss that a foothold was secured. The brave attempt was doomed to failure and, in December and January, the beaches were evacuated. The plan had failed, but a glorious page had been written in the history of Australia and New Zealand, where Anzac Day is always proudly remembered.

The port of Salonika, in Macedonia, north-east Greece, was occupied by British and French troops in October, 1915, with the object of having a possible method of entry into the enemy Balkan states. At Salonika the survivors of the Serbian Army joined the Allies, and a most difficult campaign was fought among the rugged mountains of Macedonia until the end of the war.

82

82. Lawrence of Arabia in native costume.

83. The back of a canvas and steel 'tree' observation post used on the Western front.

83

MESOPOTAMIA AND ARABIA

A glance at a map will show how the entry of Turkey into the war threatened vital British and Allied interests—the vital oil supplies at the head of the Persian Gulf, and the Suez Canal, the short sea-route to India and the Far East. The result of this threat was two separate campaigns against the Turks: one striking northwards from Basra towards Baghdad in Mesopotamia (now Iraq), and the other northwards into Palestine, in the direction of Jerusalem and Damascus. The purpose of both campaigns was the same, to drive the Turks away from two vital areas, for Syria, Palestine, Jordan and Iraq all lie immediately south of Turkey. Those countries were, therefore, the scenes of the two separate campaigns.

The campaign in Mesopotamia, the rich land between the rivers Tigris and Euphrates, centred round the city of Kut-el-Amara, which is 250 miles north of the Persian Gulf and 100 miles south of Baghdad. A British force advanced north from Basra on Baghdad, and made good progress until it was just short of the city, when it was stopped and driven back to Kut-el-Amara, where the 10,000 men were closely besieged from December, 1915, to April, 1916. During those four months, several attempts were made to relieve the beleaguered city, and more than 20,000 men were lost as a result.

The Mesopotamia campaign, in which Indian troops fought with great distinction, was complete in itself. It was hard, and costly both in casualties from battle and from sickness. It ended with the capture of Baghdad in March, 1917, which resulted in the freedom of Mesopotamia from Turkish rule, and freedom, too, from the threat to vital oil supplies.

The Arabian campaign was the scene of the great exploits of Colonel T.E. Lawrence—Lawrence of Arabia. Lawrence lived in the desert as an Arab, priding himself on being harder and tougher than the Arabs themselves. He cleverly fomented a great revolt among the Arab tribes against their Turkish rulers, and then organised them to operate in collaboration with the British army based in Egypt.

In 1917, the British army commanded by General Allenby captured Jerusalem, and then began to advance northwards. The Arab princes, led by Lawrence, advanced across the desert on Allenby's right flank and, working closely together, they captured first Damascus and then Aleppo, utterly breaking the influence of Turkey.

THE WAR IN EAST AFRICA

The German forces in German East Africa, which is now Tanganyika, were fully prepared when war broke out. A force of 260 Germans and 5,000 African troops was concentrated to make effective raids into British East Africa, now Kenya and Uganda, whilst the British military forces were, quite naturally, dispersed over a wide area. The result was that the Germans were able to strike into Kenya near Mount Kilimanjaro, where they could threaten the railway from Nairobi, the capital, to the coast at Mombasa.

The campaign was open and indecisive for the first year, as small numbers of troops operated over vast areas. The British troops were reinforced with 7,000 Indian troops, and African regiments were augmented, among them the King's African Rifles, the Gold Coast Regiment and units from Nigeria, Gambia, Cape Colony and the West Indies.

84. Three German soldiers take a rest, while a sentry and observer keep watch.

85. An American stretcher-party bringing in another casualty.

86. Arrival of a mixed bag of wounded in an American ambulance.

84

85

86

In February, 1916, General Smuts went up from South Africa to take command. Smuts had fought with great distinction against Britain in the Boer War, fifteen years earlier; now he used his fine generalship to round up the German forces and drive them back into German East Africa. Finally, he followed the retreating force into its own territory and broke it up completely.

Meanwhile, General Botha—who had also fought against Britain in the Boer War—operated against German South-West Africa and captured the territory. Thus it was that Germany lost all her colonial interests in Africa as one of the penalties for plunging the world into war.

THE WESTERN FRONT, 1918

In the meantime, there was no break from the stranglehold of trenches, wire and machine-guns on the Western Front. Every year there were major attempts to break through, and long and dreadfully costly battles; but whichever side launched the assault, however thoroughly it was prepared, and however valiantly it was finally carried out, always the defence had the last word.

The answer to the problem of trench and wire was found by Britain with the invention of the tank, an armoured fighting vehicle equipped with machine-guns, and mounted on caterpillar tracks which enabled it to break through wire and cross trenches. The story of the tank is told in the next chapter.

Germany made her final bid for victory with a massive spring offensive in March, 1918, directed against the junction of the British and French armies, between Arras and St Quentin. The objective was to separate the two armies, break through, and drive the British back to the Channel coast. The great offensive nearly succeeded, for the British line was perilously thin and there were no reserves available. The situation became so desperate that General Sir Douglas Haig issued a famous Order of the Day on April 11th:

> "There is no other course open to us but to fight it out. Every position must be held to the last man; there must be no retirement. With our backs to the wall and believing in the justice of our cause, each man must fight to the end."

The line held—thin though it was, battle-weary though every man became—until gradually the German assault spent itself, and at last a counter-attack recovered lost ground.

It was the turn of the tide. During the summer of 1918, the Allies, reinforced by fresh American troops, mounted a series of offensives supported by tanks, and wore down the German defences until, at last, in September, the final push was launched. Continuous attacks were made on every part of the German line, a succession of violent hammer-blows.

Eventually, the famous and hitherto impregnable Hindenburg Line was smashed, and the Allies advanced with ever-increasing impetus. The cavalry, after four years of fighting in the trenches as infantry, mounted their horses again. At last there was movement, eastward towards Germany. Then came the end; at eleven o'clock on the eleventh day of November, the eleventh month, the German surrender came into force and the First World War was over.

THE STORY
OF THE TANK

The problem set by the conditions on the Western Front in the autumn of 1914 was simple to state but difficult to solve. Some means had to be found by which men could cross No-man's-land through a curtain of machine-gun fire, pass through a thick barbed-wire entanglement and cross trenches. The solution was found by Britain.

THE ARMOURED CAR

The first attempt at a solution derived from the armoured car, which may be considered the ancestor of the tank. The British Expeditionary Force in France was augmented, in August 1914, by a naval brigade and a Royal Naval Air Service squadron to defend Antwerp and Dunkirk on the left of the Allied line. A hundred Rolls-Royce armoured cars were provided to protect the air bases, and to rescue pilots forced down in German territory. The cars had armour plating and a Maxim machine-gun. In December, 1914, turreted armoured cars were used. The armoured cars had electric lighting, twin rear wheels, pneumatic tyres, and detachable running-boards for use when crossing obstacles. Colonel Lawrence was very proud of his Rolls-Royce armoured car in the desert.

87. A Rolls-Royce 'Silver Ghost' armoured car in Egypt during World War I.

88. 'Mother' — the first of an ever-growing family of tanks.

87

THE FIRST TANKS

When the Royal Naval Air Service found that their armoured cars were useless against wire and trenches, they began to devise something new; they called it a "landship", and it was designed to run on caterpillar tracks. The idea was passed back to the Admiralty, where it was examined and put on one side. At the same time, a few enthusiastic Royal Engineers led by Lieutenant-Colonel Swinton were working on a similar idea, for an "armoured machine-gun destroyer". This was a modified armoured car fitted, like the "landship", with caterpillar tracks. This suggestion was passed up and was also pigeon-holed.

By good fortune there was someone of unusual vision and drive at the Admiralty, the late Winston Churchill. He saw both ideas and promptly took action by setting up a "Landship Committee".

The result was the building of the first tank, called Little Willie after the nickname given by the British troops to the Kaiser's son. Little Willie, the ancestor of all the tanks in the world, had its first trials in September, 1915. It was 28 tons, 26½ feet long, and powered by a Daimler six-cylinder sleeve-valve engine of 105 h. p. It had a speed of 3½ m.p.h., and a steering tail trailed behind. The vehicle was completely enclosed. Little Willie's balance, however, was defective and it failed in crossing obstacles.

The next design, tested in February, 1916, was first called Big Willie, then the Wilson Machine (after Lieutenant W. G. Wilson), His Majesty's Landship Centipede, and finally, and for all time—Mother. Mother was

similar mechanically to Little Willie, but her high nose gave her a greater ability for crossing obstacles. She was lozenge-shaped and her guns were mounted in sponsons on her sides. Mother's trials were held in the greatest secrecy in Hatfield Park, over an obstacle course with a replica of a German front-line trench, complete with wire, shell-holes, marshland and a five-and-a-half foot breastwork. Mother took all the obstacles splendidly.

This tank was accepted and became the prototype for a whole series, modified and improved nine times, to a total of over 2,300 machines, and it was Mother's children who bore the brunt of the fighting in France.

The Mark I, II and III had a crew of eight: commander, driver, two gearsmen and four gunners. The engine was a Daimler 105 h.p., and road speed was 3.7 m.p.h. Steering wheels were trailed, but the tracks were geared for steering as well. The tanks could clear an obstacle four-foot-six inches high, and cross a trench up to ten feet in width. The armament was two six-pounder Hotchkiss quick-firing guns and four Vickers light machine-guns. Signalling from tank to headquarters was effected by carrier pigeon, released through a small "pigeon-hole".

In action, the tanks were very hot, filled with fumes (cordite and engine exhaust), extremely noisy, and in every way uncomfortable and dangerous. Yet volunteers poured in from every branch of the Army to man the tanks in the newly-formed Tank Department, later to become the Tank Corps, then the Royal Tank Corps, and ultimately the Royal Tank Regiment.

TANKS ON THE BATTLEFIELD

The tanks were built as fast as possible, and the new tank men trained enthusiastically—all in the greatest secrecy, for this was indeed a secret weapon. In August, 1916, two companies of the Tank Department crossed to France. The vehicles were called tanks for security reasons, for when they were moved by rail or ship they were clearly labelled "water tanks for Russia", and tanks they remained.

Forty-nine tanks went into action on the Somme on the 15th September, 1916. Only eighteen actually fought; the remainder either broke down or were bogged down in the terrible Flanders mud. But the eighteen made history. As they lurched and rumbled across No-man's-land, their guns firing, smashing down barbed wire and crossing trenches, the British infantry, so long bedevilled by wire and machine-guns, cheered wildly. The tanks terrified the startled German infantry, who gazed at them in astonishment and fled.

At general headquarters, a message was dropped by an aeroplane: "*A tank is walking up High Street at Flers with the British army cheering behind*". Flers was behind the enemy line, and until then quite unapproachable. The tank had made its entry on the stage of war and battle was never to be the same again. Sir Douglas Haig ordered a thousand tanks, and new models were built—the Mark IV, Mark V and the Whippet.

TANKS AT CAMBRAI

After the first excitement, critics raised their voices. They were not convinced that the tank was really a valuable weapon; they pointed to the fact that nearly two-thirds of the force used on the Somme failed, and that the success, though spectacular, led to no serious penetration of the enemy line. The tank enthusiasts replied that the mud of the Somme was not tank country, and that no proper support had been arranged.

The tanks were given another chance, on the ground of their own choosing and with their own tactical support, in November, 1917, at the Battle of Cambrai.

The ground was relatively smooth to give good going to tanks, and most careful plans were made for an assault on the heavily fortified and defended Hindenburg Line. Nine tank battalions were to be used, consisting of 380 fighting and 100 administrative tanks. The tanks were to advance in three waves without the customary preliminary bombardment, supported by six divisions of infantry, two cavalry divisions and a thousand guns. The infantry were to advance in file behind the tanks, which would clear gaps in the wire, silence machine-gun posts and cross the trenches, while the infantry mopped up and secured captured positions. The leading tanks carried fascines of brushwood on their noses, to drop into the enemy trenches to facilitate crossing.

The advance began at six in the morning, and by four in the afternoon a penetration of ten thousand yards had been made on thirteen thousand yards of heavily-defended front. The booty was eight thousand prisoners and a hundred guns. The battle itself failed to achieve its main objectives, through exhaustion of the attacking infantry and tank crews, and lack of supporting divisions, but the tank men had proved their point, and had shown the way to final victory in the following year.

DEVELOPMENT BETWEEN THE WARS

After the war, tank development became the concern of every country. In Britain development was hampered by the Government's unwillingness to spare money for research in armaments. War Office policy was to develop three distinct types of tank, on the same principle as warships— light for reconnaissance, medium or cruiser as fighting machines with rapid mobility, and heavy for making an initial break-through in close

TOP: Sappers opening the way through the minefields at the Battle of El Alamein on the night of 23rd October, 1942, from the painting by Terence Cuneo.

BOTTOM: Decisive breakthrough at Omaha Beach by American troops on D-Day, from the film 'The Longest Day'.

co-operation with the infantry. By 1939 the three types were in supply—the Vickers Light Tank, the Vickers Cruiser (superseded by the Christie), and the Matilda II heavy tank, followed next year by the Valentine.

It is interesting to compare the progress made by Britain, America, Russia and Germany in heavy tanks by 1940.

GREAT BRITAIN	WEIGHT	CREW	ARMAMENT
Valentine	17 tons	3	2-pounder
			1 heavy machine-gun
AMERICA			
Lee and Grant	30 tons	5	1 75-mm.
			1 37-mm.
			1 machine-gun
			(Lee, 2 machine-guns)
RUSSIA			
KV I	46 tons	5	1 76-mm.
			3 machine-guns
GERMANY			
Panzerkampf-wagen IV	23 tons	5	1 75-mm.
			2 machine-guns

Nothing stimulates development of weapons like war, and the Second World War of 1939–1945 saw great developments in tank design, speed and fire-power. The following table gives basic details of tanks in use in each of the above countries at the end of the war.

GREAT BRITAIN	WEIGHT	CREW	ARMAMENT
Centurion	48 tons	4	17-pounder
			1 machine-gun
AMERICA			
Pershing	38–41 tons	5	1 90-mm.
			3 machine-guns
RUSSIA			
JS III	46 tons	4	1 122-mm.
			2 machine-guns
GERMANY			
Tiger II	67 tons	5	1 88-mm.
			2 machine-guns

THE TANK MEN

The development of the tank as a primary weapon was necessarily accompanied by the formation of tanks corps to fight them. After World War I, the British Tank Corps became the Royal Tank Regiment, with the distinctive black beret, the most convenient head-dress in a tank. The coming of the tank solved another teasing problem—what to do with the cavalry regiments when horses had no place in modern war. The answer, of course, was to replace the horses with armoured cars or tanks. In 1928 the revolutionary step was taken of converting two cavalry regiments—the 11th Hussars and the 12th Lancers—to armoured car regiments.

The effect of this on men whose whole lives centred round their horses and horsemanship can well be imagined. The process was continued and,

A forward observation party awaiting evacuation by helicopter.

89. Russian tanks advancing on a German aero
drome at Jdanske.

90. This Sherman 'Crab' is one example o
'The Funnies' introduced during World War I

by 1939, all the British cavalry regiments, except the Household Cavalry, were converted to armoured car or tank regiments. A new corps was formed, the Royal Armoured Corps, consisting of the cavalry regiments and the Royal Tank Regiment. The Household Cavalry kept their horses for ceremonial occasions, but were trained to fight in armoured cars.

Every army carried out reorganisations of a similar kind, so that the cavalry tradition was transferred to the new weapon.

TANKS AT WAR

Britain had invented the tank, but it was Germany who developed the technique of using the new weapon to the best advantage. When the Nazi Party, led by Adolf Hitler, came to power in Germany in 1933, the national policy was based squarely on military power. A large army was quickly mustered, and German industry and mechanical skill were directed to equipping it with the most modern weapons in vast quantities. Driven by the totalitarian authority of a dictatorship, Germany armed, and her men drilled and trained, with a fervour verging on the hysterical.

Hitler's aggressions in Europe—Austria in 1938, Czechoslovakia and Poland in 1939—were spearheaded not by marching armies, but long columns of tanks. When the Germans invaded France and Belgium in 1940, as they had done in 1914, it was with the newly-invented technique of *Blitzkrieg*—lightning war. Massive formations of fast and powerfully armoured tanks advanced in columns, closely supported by dive-bombing aircraft, and punched their way through all opposition. Commanders, officers and crews of the tanks were thoroughly trained and exercised, and the tanks struck, indeed, like lightning, sweeping all before them.

91. Member of a German tank-crew surrenders to a British infantryman in the Western Desert.

92. Nearly 50 years after 'Mother' comes the 'Chieftain', Britain's most up-to-date tank.

Throughout the war, tanks played a vital part, restoring the mobility which the trench and wire systems had destroyed. New tactics of attack and defence were evolved, to make the best use of the mobility and fire-power of the armoured divisions.

Every new weapon produces counter-measures: the arrow—armour; the machine-gun—the trench and pillbox; and the tank—anti-tank mines and anti-tank guns. At the Battle of El Alamein, in 1942, sappers advanced first, clearing paths through the German minefields for the tanks, whilst the infantry concentrated on enemy anti-tank guns.

Once cavalry trotted into action, fine manes tossing, accoutrements a-jingle—now great steel monsters rumble along, their gun barrels threatening, the radio sets crackling and buzzing.

"THE FUNNIES"

Tanks were adapted during World War II for special purposes; the British troops called them "The Funnies". Flail tanks were fitted with a revolving drum in front, from which lengths of chain flailed the ground to set off land-mines. Fascine tanks carried special material to be dropped into ditches to make a footing. Bridging tanks carried bridge spans, sometimes to lay them across a ditch, sometimes to sit in the ditch themselves so that other tanks could cross the bridge on top. The D. D. (Duplex Drive) tank was an American Sherman, specially modified so that it could be launched from a ship up to four miles out at sea, and swim ashore to climb on to the beach under its own power.

Self-propelled guns were widely used: guns mounted on a tank chassis, so that they could move without any other traction.

BETWEEN
THE WARS

The great majority of the millions of soldiers of all nations who had fought in World War I were civilians, and when at last the war ended, those who had been fortunate enough to survive took off their uniforms with immense relief and went back to civilian life. The overwhelming sense of relief engendered a deep desire so to arrange things that there should never be another war. From that desire the League of Nations was created. This was intended to be a league, or parliament, of all the nations, where international disputes would be settled by discussion, and where everyone would work together with good will to preserve world peace. It was a splendid ideal but, tragically, it was doomed to failure.

The disaster which brought war again in twenty years came from the growth of two powerful dictatorships, in Italy and in Germany. One was the Italian Fascist Party, led by Benito Mussolini, who came to power in 1922, and the other was the German Nazi Party, formed by Adolf Hitler, who became Chancellor in 1933. An essential of a dictatorship is military strength, and therein lay the danger to peace; bold and arrogant government, backed by a large and well-equipped army, is a permanent threat to other nations, and so it proved.

Italy was the first dictatorship and set the pattern which was copied in a more deadly manner later by Germany. *Il Duce*, or The Leader, as Mussolini styled himself, delighted in impressive parades with bands and banners, rank upon rank of stern-looking troops giving the Fascist salute, while great crowds of proud civilians cheered. Italy, Mussolini loudly claimed, was the heir to Imperial Rome. And like Imperial Rome, modern Italy needed conquest.

ITALY'S CONQUEST OF ETHIOPIA

Ethiopia, the chosen victim for Fascist conquest, was a wild and rugged kingdom with no industry and a simple, peasant way of life. It has a long and a proud history and is still ruled by the Emperor who is also styled "The King of Kings of Ethiopia, Lion of Judah, Elect of God". It is situated in East Africa and, at the time in question, it had Italian Eritrea on its northern border, and Italian Somaliland on its eastern frontier.

The only pretext for Italy's assault was an old and unimportant dispute over some frontier wells. Italy made careful preparations and, as supply ships passed down the Suez Canal to establish bases on the Ethiopian frontier, the threatened nation reported the situation to the League of Nations. But the only results were moving speeches, and the imposition of sanctions by which neither party to the dispute could be supplied with arms or ammunition. As Italy was already fully prepared, this only prevented Ethiopia from getting weapons for her own defence. So much for the dreams of the power of the League of Nations.

93. A group of Polish insurgents at the time of the uprising in 1919.

94. A cavalry patrol of General Chiang Kai-Shek's army in Canton, 1925.

95. Abyssinian troops defending Addis Ababa from the advancing Italian Army.

96. Italian troops marching through Rome before embarking for Abyssinia.

93

94

The Italian Army invaded Ethiopia on October 3rd, 1935; it was the first event of the tragic series which was eventually to plunge more than half the world into war four years later. The contest was pathetically unequal. The Ethiopian Army was small and poorly equipped; its white-robed cavalry were brilliant horsemen, but its tactics were primitive and its only weapons old-fashioned carbines. The Italian Army had trained for many years and had all the modern weapons: artillery, machine-guns, tanks and aircraft. The Ethiopians' only advantage was the wildness of their country and the righteousness of the cause.

Small, simple villages were dive-bombed and machine-gunned. Towns were sprayed with mustard gas from the air. The Ethiopians fought in their mountains, sniping from craggy vantage points, stalking the enemy after dark. But it was an easy conquest and, after six months, the Italian Army marched triumphantly into the capital, Addis Ababa. The Emperor found sanctuary in Britain, whilst the King of Italy was proclaimed Emperor of Abyssinia, and Mussolini wore the laurels of the conqueror.

NAZI GERMANY

The main danger to the peace of Europe was not Italy, however, but Germany. Italians are not warlike by nature, and the Fascist parades and talk of Imperial Rome were mainly a façade. Germany was quite a different proposition, with a military tradition of long standing. The Germans have always produced good soldiers, willing to submit to iron discipline. When Hitler told them that man was a natural fighting animal, and a nation a fighting unit, their martial instincts were stirred.

Conscription was introduced in Germany in 1935, in direct opposition to the Peace Treaty of 1919, and an army of half a million was raised. This was continually increased, by further conscription and by the constant flow of enthusiastic young volunteers. They brought their traditional loyalty and devotion to the Nazi badge, the black swastika in a white ring on a red background, as their fathers had brought it to the Imperial German eagle. The German people considered themselves the "master race", and they were eager to prove it to the world.

Hitler, the *Führer* (or Leader) was the complete master of Germany, supported by an ever-growing army and a very large secret police. German industry, always clever, was geared to producing arms and equipment. Germany became intoxicated by its Fuhrer's wild speeches and ambitions, and Europe's dreams of perpetual peace melted away.

THE SPANISH CIVIL WAR

The first war to break out within Europe was, however, not caused by either of the dictators. It was the civil war which broke out in Spain in 1936. On one side was the Republican Government, which had come to power in place of the monarchy in 1931, and on the other was the Army, led by General Franco and backed by the well-to-do classes and the Church, who resented the left-wing policies of the new government. General Franco professed fascist principles, and consequently received much sympathy from Germany and Italy.

The European nations, including Germany and Italy, agreed on a policy of non-intervention, to keep the war from spreading beyond Spain. Nevertheless, Germany permitted thousands of "volunteers" to go to Spain to assist Franco, all of them specialists or technicians, who were thus able to test their aircraft, guns or tanks in active service conditions. Italy sent five complete divisions of fully-equipped "volunteers", and later aug-

97

98

7. French troops await the arrival of an ammunition train, in a gallery of the Maginot Line.

8. Japanese columns marching past a British post at Shanghai during the Sino-Japanese War.

9. Chinese soldiers in action against the Japanese invaders.

mented them to the strength of a full army corps. An International Brigade of many nationalities went to fight for the Republicans, and the U.S.S.R., asked for help, sent her contribution in men and weapons.

In the main, however, it was a war of Spaniard against Spaniard, and, as always with civil wars, it was a savage and murderous conflict. Franco fought with the normal military formations, but the Republicans fought mainly as "guerrillas", often living in small communities in mountain fastnesses, with no uniforms beyond perhaps an arm-band or a beret worn as a sign of allegiance. The Insurgents were properly organised and trained soldiers, with headquarters, customary ranks and types of unit, a supply system, and medical services. Their unofficial allies from Germany and Italy were also regular soldiers.

The Republicans had none of these advantages. They were loosely organised in small bands, usually based in the mountains, where they lived hard. They used what weapons they could get, often procured by raiding the enemy. They had no supply system, and treatment for their wounded was difficult if not impossible to obtain. Their tactics were the ambush, the sudden raid, and the destruction of bridges and vital points. Women fought with the men, and cooked and cared for them.

Spain was torn by war for three dreadful years until, gradually, the better organisation and weapons of Franco's troops gained the ascendancy, ending in final triumph in 1939. A fascist government was set up with Franco at the head. With a final burst of vengeance, the Republicans were hunted from their hiding-places and the civil war ended. It had been ruthless and cruel, with deeds of horror and heroism by both sides.

WAR BETWEEN JAPAN AND CHINA

The militant spirit and the ambition for conquest which flourished in Germany and Italy were matched at the other side of the world by Japan. The Japanese Army, highly trained and equipped with all modern weapons, was supported by a very powerful navy. Japan also had dreams and visions of greatness, enforced by arms. It was towards China that Japan looked for her conquest.

China was the contrast to Japan in many important features. Japan was industrial, skilled with modern techniques and ambitious; China was principally agricultural, her population mainly peasant, and she was peaceable. In 1931, Japan began her policy of aggression against China, using a minor pretext to invade at the northern end of the Yellow Sea. The city of Mukden, now Shenyang, was soon captured, also the vital section of the Manchurian railway. The Japanese made swift and easy

99

progress, for the Chinese lacked anti-tank guns, aircraft or, indeed, any weapons to match the invader's. China's only asset was the great numbers of men on which she could draw and their splendid spirit of resistance. But mere numbers and bravery are not sufficient to stop an enemy with better weapons, and the Japanese were able to advance deep into Manchuria until it fell entirely into their hands, with the Chinese driven back to the Great Wall of China on the western borders of the province.

A lull followed. A League of Nations Commission went to restore peace, but Japan had shown that "Might is Right" and she held fast to her conquest while planning the next move. But a new spirit had been aroused in China; political differences within the country were dropped in the face of common danger and, under General Chiang Kai-shek, she organised her military strength. Young Chinese drilled and trained, adapting ancient, traditional ways to the usages of modern warfare.

Japan attacked China again in 1936, overrunning the whole district around Peking and Tientsin and advancing deep into the interior. The government moved six hundred miles south of Peking to Nankow, and Chinese life became centred in the mountains to the north-west, where supplies could be obtained from the outside world, via Siberia and the Burma Road.

The war lasted nine years. The Japanese used their aircraft in support of tanks, and tried to break the spirit of China by bombing schools, hospitals and universities. Where they engaged the Chinese, their better weapons gave them the advantage, but China is a vast land, and her people fought with dogged perseverance. It was a complicated campaign, ranging far and wide over plains and mountains, but the Japanese could never bring the Chinese to final defeat, however often they won individual engagements; their control never extended beyond the immediate range of their weapons. The war merged into World War II, and ended only in 1945 with the utter defeat of Japan.

THE MAGINOT LINE

Mussolini had declared that events in Europe turned on the Rome-Berlin "Axis", and this was given a world-wide significance when Japan joined the European dictators. The threat to European and world peace caused by the belligerence of these three countries was evident to all. France took steps to secure herself from the German threat by building mighty defences along her German frontier, adapting the ancient principle of defence by strong fortresses to the age of high explosives and aerial bombardment.

The Maginot Line was a wonderful feat of modern engineering. It stretched northwards along the German frontier from Switzerland to Luxembourg, and ended on the Belgian frontier. It was a complicated system of steel and concrete underground fortresses, with hundreds of miles of connecting passages, magazines and accommodation; powerful lifts raised heavy guns to ground level for firing. The country in front was ruthlessly cleared and levelled, and thickly defended along its entire length with anti-tank obstacles and minefields.

The Maginot Line also provided defence in depth. Two miles in front was another line of strongpoints, the *Ligne d'Arrêt*, six miles in front again was the *Ligne de Recul*, on which the defenders of the foremost line could fall back, and a further four miles forward was the *Ligne de Contact*, where the enemy would be first engaged. This whole intricate defence system was as strong as modern science could make it, and it seemed to be quite invulnerable. There was in this an inherent danger, because France was

100. Steel-helmeted German infantry entering Austria at the time of the annexation, in 1938

101. Following the introduction of conscription in Britain, Militiamen went into training in the summer of 1939.

100

101

lulled into a false feeling of security which permitted Hitler to reach for more and more power in Europe.

The Maginot Line was matched inside the German frontier by the Siegfried Line, or West Wall of Germany. This too was a formidable defensive line of steel and concrete, constructed with all the skill of modern military engineering. It was, however, little more than a gesture, for Hitler had other plans and the Siegfried Line was never completed.

THE GROWTH OF GERMAN POWER

One of Hitler's main advantages in leading the German people was their understandable anger at the restrictions laid upon them at the Treaty of Versailles after World War I. The victorious Allies, also understandably, made Germany agree to severe limitations of arms. The Rhineland, between the Rhine and the Belgian frontier, was demilitarised, to avoid, it was hoped, a repetition of Germany's invasion of Belgium in 1914.

In 1936, Hitler made his first great gamble; he marched troops across the Rhine into the Rhineland. It was a decisive moment in history; would French troops be ordered into the Rhineland to drive the Germans back? But the Western Powers were pledged to avoid war, and no more than a few French troops were sent up to the Maginot Line. Hitler's gamble had succeeded, and Germany occupied the Rhineland. That was the first step.

With this success behind him, Hitler turned to Austria and, in 1938, made a bloodless conquest. Nazi flags were hung out, and the Austrians, except for those who dared to stay indoors and risk the attentions of the police, welcomed the German columns and troops. Britain and France protested, talked to Hitler, and tried to bring sanity without war.

But Hitler was already waging a ghastly war within Germany, and extending it to each new territory he conquered by ruthless political and military scheming. This war was a completely one-sided racial purge of the Jewish people, who were first treated as slaves and later put to death, after suffering unspeakably, in concentration camps.

By 1945, millions of European Jews had been systematically destroyed by the Nazis, whose special party troops were employed to hound, torture and kill innocent men, women and children, not only of Jewish origin but of many different nationalities besides. It was this racial and political persecution which set Hitler aside from all the dictators of history as the most evil menace to world-wide civilisation which had ever arisen.

Meanwhile, the military explosion was coming closer and closer, as crisis after crisis shook Europe.

With Austria joined to Germany on the southern section of her eastern frontier, Hitler turned to Czechoslovakia in the centre, and after long months of political intrigue, threats, guarantees and promises, Germany annexed Czechoslovakia in 1939. There remained Poland in the north, the buffer state between Germany and Russia. Policies of pacificism and appeasement in Britain and France began to lose much of their support. Britain plunged into a programme of rearmament. As the familiar German propaganda machine directed its attentions on Poland, the course of future events became quite clear, and Britain and France added warnings to their words of protest. They stated that if Germany attacked Poland, both Britain and France would go to her aid.

Germany was not to be deterred. The West had talked a great deal for a long time, but Hitler's progress had not been halted. On September 1st, 1939, German troops, tanks and aircraft attacked Poland. Her lines of communication were shattered by bombing attacks, dive-bombers tore gaps in the defences, and columns of tanks—the best in the world—led the German Army into Poland.

Poland is a land with a great military tradition, but her gallant resistance was of no avail against the deadly efficiency of the new Nazi war-machine. Before help could reach her from the west, she was overwhelmed.

Two days after the invasion of Poland, Britain and France declared war on Germany. Australia, New Zealand, Canada and South Africa followed Britain's lead. Belgium remained neutral. France manned the Maginot Line and loaded the guns. In Britain and the Commonwealth, the navies, air forces and armies prepared for battle; troops were mobilised. Twenty years after the "war to end war", World War II broke out.

102. Men of the Cheshire Regiment training with a machine-gun on the range at Aldershot, four months before the outbreak of the Second World War.

102

THE SECOND
WORLD WAR

In September, 1939, "the lights went out in Europe"; windows were blacked-out with shutters or dark curtains so that not a chink of light would help to guide an enemy bomber. No street or public lights were permitted; car headlamps were masked. Air-raid shelters were dug, and Air Raid Precautions introduced. Gas-masks were issued; children took them to school, and babies were given a special kind. It was total war.

For the first six months, however, nothing happened in France, where French and British armies faced the Germans. The French stood on guard in the Maginot Line, and the British Expeditionary Force was in position along the Franco-Belgian frontier. The German Siegfried Line was also manned, and everyone waited. They called it the "Phoney War".

The soldiers who had fought in France during World War I wore a khaki tunic, leather belt, puttees wound round the legs, and a peaked cap. In

103. German cycle battalion passing through Oslo, following the invasion of Norway.

104. After Dunkirk, Britain's Channel coast became a forward line of defence.

World War II, they wore battle-dress—an easier and more efficient uniform with the blouse buttoned to the trousers—a webbing belt, webbing gaiters, and a forage cap or a steel helmet.

GERMAN ATTACK IN FRANCE

The "Phoney War" ended with startling suddenness in April, 1940, when Germany invaded Denmark and Norway. Then, in May, Hitler turned on Holland, bombing Rotterdam and killing 30,000 people; simultaneously, he invaded Belgium and, on May 10th, 1940, the British Expeditionary Force advanced swiftly across the country to the River Dyle, in an attempt to stop the invaders. But the new German method of war, the *Blitzkrieg*, swept all before it. Heavy dive-bombing attacks cleared the way for the fast-moving armoured columns of tanks, which were followed by lorried infantry.

By attacking through Belgium, the Germans had outflanked the elaborate Maginot Line and rendered it useless. German columns smashed through the French front between Namur and Sedan, and the B.E.F. were thus forced to fall back to the Escaut, and then to their original positions on the Franco-Belgian frontier. By May 28th, the Germans had reached the Channel near Abbeville, and four days later the Belgian Army surrendered. With both flanks gone, the B.E.F., already battle-weary and bewildered by the speed of these disasters, had to make a fighting retreat to Dunkirk. A defensive perimeter was formed, and 225,000 British and 112,000 Allied soldiers escaped to England, rescued under fire by a unique fleet of ships from destroyers to yachts, and paddle-steamers to river-craft.

The survivors were a sad remnant of the well-equipped and confident B.E.F. which had crossed to France. They were exhausted and ragged; many were wounded. 13,000 had been killed, 40,000 had become prisoners of war. The material losses were 700 tanks, 2,400 guns and 50,000 vehicles. The last survivors reached England on June 3rd, and a week later the British force which had gone to Norway, six weeks before, came home too. France surrendered on June 16th and, soon afterwards, Hitler danced with joy on the edge of the English Channel. Kaiser Wilhelm had failed to break through to the Channel in four years; Hitler was there in five weeks. only Britain remained—a weakly defended island across the narrow sea.

Britain and the Commonwealth stood alone; many governments and people believed that Britain would swiftly fall, as all the other nations had, before the military might of Germany. Not so the British people, now led by Winston Churchill, nor the French who had escaped to continue the fight. Britain became a fortress island: beaches were mined and defended by wire, strongpoints with guns occupied every good defensive site. The signal that invasion had commenced was to be the ringing of the church bells throughout the land. Men too old or too young to serve, or those engaged in essential industry joined the Home Guard (at first called Local Defence Volunteers), and drilled in their spare time. They manned church towers and hill-tops, armed with shot-guns, on watch for German parachutists. Elderly officers sometimes served as private soldiers.

But the Germans did not invade England. The invasion barges were collected, and the assault troops stood ready, while the Luftwaffe flew over the Channel to destroy the Royal Air Force, as a necessary prelude to invasion. The Battle of Britain, however, was won by the R.A.F., and Hitler turned his attention to the ruthless bombing of cities. London suffered 20,000 killed, the centre of Coventry was obliterated, and every major

A map of the general position in Europe during World War II.

05. The alarm sounds in a bunker of Germany's West Wall during the early days of the war.

06. Members of the House of Lords L.D.V. unit receive musketry instruction in July, 1940.

07. Typical infantryman of the Wehrmacht.

08. Mopping up 'pockets' of Italian troops during the British advance in Libya.

town was attacked. But in October, 1940, the R.A.F. shot down 2,375 German aircraft for the loss of 700. Hitler, deprived of air-superiority, withdrew his invasion army from the French coast; fortress Britain remained uninvaded and unconquered.

ITALY AT WAR

In the spring of 1940, when Hitler seemed invincible, Italy entered the war. She had made an easy conquest of Albania in April, 1939, and in October, 1940, her third act of aggression was launched. This time, however, events turned out differently from Mussolini's expectations. Using Albania as a base, the Italian Army marched into Greece, whereupon the smaller Greek Army drove it back over the frontier, and then inflicted a resounding defeat on the invader well inside Albanian territory.

A more important result of Italy's declaration of war was the situation in North Africa. Italy possessed Libya, which lies between Tunisia and Egypt. The British Eighth Army was stationed in Egypt to protect the Suez Canal. With the Axis powers dominating the Mediterranean, Britain was cut off from the short route to India. Only the two strongholds of Gibraltar and Malta stood in the path of complete control by Hitler and Mussolini.

In November, 1940, a strong Italian army advanced eastwards from Libya with the object of seizing Egypt. The British Eighth Army, much inferior in numbers, promptly drove the Italians back, taking 300,000 prisoners and occupying Libya. Germany at once went to the rescue of her ally with the Afrika Korps, a force of a very different quality from the Italian Army and flushed with Germany's triumphs in Europe.

The Eighth Army was depleted by the transfer of divisions to Greece, to help her against overwhelming German attacks; when, therefore, the Afrika Korps attacked, the Eighth Army was driven back three hundred miles towards Egypt. Like a pendulum, the battle swung westwards again with the British offensive of November, 1941, and then, in June, 1942, swung in favour of the Germans. The Eighth Army now stood on a line south from El Alamein, guarding the way to Egypt and the Suez Canal.

The desert armies developed special characteristics. Dress was khaki drill—either shorts or trousers, and an open-necked shirt. Both sides had one common enemy—thirst. It was open warfare on the rolling desert, with few towns or villages to be ruined. As a result of this, the problem of coping with hordes of pathetic civilian refugees, homeless and lost, which faced the armies in Europe, scarcely arose at all. It was a war with hot days and cold nights, with flies and but little comfort. The great distances made the armies dependent on their tanks and armoured cars, trucks and field cars. Everything depended on two vital commodities: petrol for the vehicles and water for the men.

The battle of El Alamein in October, 1942, proved to be the turning-point of the war in Europe. It was the first major victory over the Germans, and it marked the turn of the tide. By that time, the United States had come into the war and, while the battle was being fought, mighty convoys were taking a combined British and American assault force to Morocco and Algeria, at the other end of North Africa. The plan was to attack the Axis from east and west, and so squeeze them out of Africa.

The Battle of El Alamein lasted twelve days, a violent struggle between two highly experienced and determined armies, the one commanded by General Montgomery, the other by Field-Marshal Rommel. Eventually, the Axis line was broken, and the Eighth Army began a twelve-hundred-mile pursuit, fighting German rearguards whenever they could make

109. Battle scene during the defence of Brest Litovsk by the surrounded Russian garrison.

110. Cavalry —still employed at times by the Russians in the Second World War —thunder into the attack.

111. American assault troops making a fresh breach in the defences of Hitler's vaunted European fortress.

a stand. At the same time, the American-British army was fighting eastwards towards Tunis. In April, 1943, the two armies met in Tunisia, and the Axis armies in North Africa surrendered. Egypt was safe and the whole of the southern Mediterranean coast was in Allied hands.

The Axis had to be attacked in Europe, and North Africa provided the ideal base. Gigantic combined operations were planned; in July and September, 1943, British and American landings were made in Sicily, and at Salerno on the Italian coast south of Naples. Before the Salerno landings took place, Mussolini's government was overthrown, and Italy became an ally of Britain, France and America.

For two years the Allies fought their way northwards up Italy, with its spine of mountains and its many lateral rivers. Beautiful towns were devastated by battle, as aircraft bombed and tanks smashed their way forward. In the summer heat troops wore khaki drill, in the cold winters they needed thick clothing. At times the mountain fighting was so difficult that only mules could penetrate to positions with supplies. The Germans chose a series of defensive lines, each of which had to be assaulted in turn. But inexorably the American Fifth and the British Eighth Armies fought forward until, in 1945, they broke through the last defensive line in the broad valley of the River Po, and Italy was won.

THE RUSSIAN FRONT

In June, 1941, Hitler turned eastwards, having failed in his plans to invade Britain, and attacked Russia. The preparations were made with typical German efficiency, and mighty armies of heavy tanks, guns and lorried infantry rumbled eastwards, supported by the *Luftwaffe*. The great attack had such impetus that in a few months the Russian armies, fighting desperately and courageously, were driven back to a line which ran right across Russia for a thousand miles, from Leningrad in the Gulf of Finland to Rostov on the Sea of Azov, passing within thirty miles of Moscow and through the very suburbs of Stalingrad (now called Volgograd).

The spectacular success of the German armies was marred by the fact that they now had very long lines of communications for bringing up supplies, and by the severity of the Russian winter. When the iron cold closed down, with frequent blizzards sweeping across a white world of snow, the German soldiers suffered terribly, for the assault had been planned as a swift campaign, and no winter clothing had been provided.

The crisis of the battle for Russia came in December, 1941, with Leningrad and Stalingrad closely besieged, and the battle for Moscow itself raging within thirty miles north, west and south of the city. Russian heroism rose to the greatest heights. The imagination of the whole world was captured by the long fight to defend Stalingrad. The citizens, men, women and boys, manned positions amongst the debris of the suburbs, and fought with passionate devotion to save their city; surrender was never considered. Life was harsh and death ever-present. The world marvelled as the Red Army and the citizens of Stalingrad kept the large German army at bay. The siege lasted from July, 1942, until February, 1943.

Stalingrad became a double battle. While the German Sixth Army fought to capture the city in the face of the fanatical defence, a brilliant pincer-movement was effected by two Russian armies, which surrounded the German force, cutting it off from all supplies and reinforcements. Another German army went to the rescue, but could not break the iron ring forged by the Red Army. For two months, in the depths of the winter of 1942 to 1943, the great battle was waged. The end came when the German

Sixth Army was annihilated and Stalingrad relieved. The Red Army's prisoners included 24 generals, 2,500 officers and 91,000 other ranks.

Throughout 1943, the great battles of the Eastern Front continued. Russia was supplied from industries established far in the rear, and by convoys from Britain which braved the voyage through the submarine-infested northern waters. In October and November, 1943, the tide turned, when the Red Army drove right through the German line to capture Kiev. With their northern and southern armies separated, the Germans had to fall back. Leningrad was relieved and, with gathering impetus, the Red Army forced the invaders back until they were clear of Russian soil. Then they fought on towards Germany itself.

The casualties suffered by both sides on the Eastern Front were immense, numbered by the million. It was a harsh campaign, and the suffering of the German troops in the Russian winters was terrible.

THE NORMANDY LANDINGS

While the Red Army was beating the Germans back from Russia, and the American and British armies were driving them up Italy, Europe was assaulted in the west. An immense American-British landing was made on the Normandy beaches in June, 1944. Five British and three American brigades crossed from England and forced the heavily fortified beaches, establishing a bridgehead through which the follow-up troops could be put ashore. The prefabricated Mulberry Harbour was towed across the Channel to facilitate the disembarkation of men and stores. With the invasion army was a small Free French contingent, composed of Frenchmen who had escaped at Dunkirk or who had slipped across afterwards. Their commander was General de Gaulle.

Germany was now under attack from the east, south and west. The lessons taught by the German *blitzkrieg* of 1940 had been well learnt, and now the Allies thrust forward under heavy air support, with columns of fast tanks possessing great fire-power. Eleven months of violent fighting ensued, as the battle was waged across France and towards Germany.

The end came in May, 1945, five years after the Germans had attacked Belgium and France. On the 2nd of the month the German forces in Italy surrendered, and on the 7th the entire German forces by land, sea and air, surrendered unconditionally. Hitler and a few of his closest companions committed suicide in their bomb-proof headquarters in Berlin. Allied and Russian troops marched into Berlin. The lights went on in Europe.

RESISTANCE AND LIBERATION MOVEMENTS

In every country overrun by the Germans there were men, and women, too, who refused to accept defeat. They devoted their lives to harming the enemy in any way they could. They lived dangerously and went in constant risk of torture and death by the German secret police, the dreaded Gestapo. They lived normal law-abiding lives outwardly, while they worked in secret to sabotage factories or bridges, to collect information which was sent to Britain by secret radio transmitters, and to assist the Allies in any way they could.

Special trained resistance workers were parachuted into Europe by night, to organise groups for special tasks. Weapons and explosives were also dropped by parachute in lonely fields, where men and women waited to snatch them up and hide them away. Messages were sent in code by the

112

113

12. German troops passing burning oilfields in the U.S.S.R.

13. Sniper-hunting Canadians during street-fighting in Italy.

COLOUR PLATES

ABOVE: An Honest John rocket pictured on its launching-pad.

RIGHT: Fuelling a Corporal guided missile.

BELOW: Operator at the controls of a new radar system for the rapid location of enemy mortar positions.

ABOVE: A forward Scatter/Radar communication site, U. S. Army.

BELOW: American soldier seen working on Nike missile.

TOP RIGHT: The R. A. S. C. Launch 'Flying Fox' at Kingston, Jamaica.

BOTTOM RIGHT: Preparing parachutes for army supply-dropping operation in the jungle

TOP: Members of the catering corps serving food to soldiers on exercises in Cyprus.

BOTTOM: Army medical services not only care for the health of the troops, but also for that of their families.

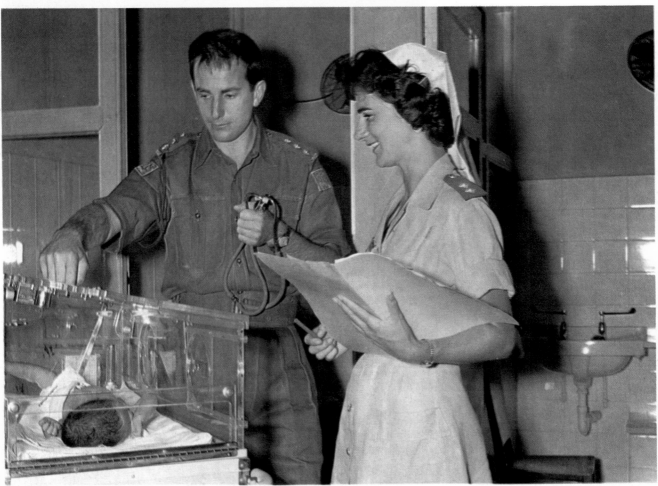

B.B.C., and many a mild-looking tradesman, business girl or school-teacher was proud to risk the terrible penalty of discovery.

The partisans formed into bands and fought as guerrillas, fighting the Germans as independent units. They were brave and desperate men—and there were often women among them—who fought in secret and with deadly efficiency. In the mountains of Italy and Yugoslavia, in the wilder parts of France, wherever there was concealment, the partisans operated against the occupying Germans. They were well armed and equipped with grenades and explosives, sometimes dropped by parachute from Allied aircraft, sometimes stolen from the Germans.

Partisan units used their knowledge of the terrain, and the daring and skill of the individual soldier, to ambush German, Italian and other Axis troops, to raid their headquarters, to cut lines of communication, and to destroy enemy forces and their equipment in any way they could.

YUGOSLAV WAR OF LIBERATION

The Yugoslav partisans were exceptionally well organised and successful, perhaps the supreme example of the enormous part played by resistance and liberation movements during the Second World War.

After the occupation of Yugoslavia by the Axis powers, the country was divided up between Germany, Italy, Hungary and Bulgaria. Some regions were annexed, others occupied, and a "puppet" State of Croatia was brought into being.

Everywhere, the foreign conquerors and their allies—such as Ustashi and other quislings—despoiled the country and tried to enslave the Yugoslavs. Frequently, they went further still, playing on political and religious

14. D-Day casualties receive attention as fresh troops storm ashore.

15. Yugoslav Partisans lay an ambush.

16. Beach-head foxholes occupied by American soldiers during the initial assault on D-Day.

17. By tearing up the track, Yugoslav Partisans disrupt German communications.

beliefs and differences to disunite the people. Led by the Communist Party of Yugoslavia, which after the invasion of Axis troops was the only organised political force in the country, Yugoslavs rebelled against the invaders and quislings. After careful preparations, thousands of patriots took up arms and joined partisan units, determined to defend their homes and families, and to fight for the liberation of their country.

Within a few months of the invasion in April, 1941, a countrywide network of partisan detachments had been created, together with a Main Headquarters which co-ordinated the struggle of the nation. Inspired by their leader, Marshal Tito, Yugoslav partisans endured terrible hardships, fighting against powerful and numerically far superior enemy forces.

Without transport, regular rations of food, or any of the advantages of a regular army, the men marched and fought in all weathers, aware that they could not rely on normal medical help, or supplies of arms and food.

Alertness, physical endurance, individual initiative, adaptability and absolute loyalty to the struggle for freedom were the predominant qualities called for in every partisan.

His will to carry on in the face of frightful odds was reinforced by the crying need of his countrymen; and his efforts were given greater strength and urgency when, all about him, he saw the atrocities committed against women, children and old people.

The citizens, and the villagers of the country regions, did all in their power to maintain the Partisan Detachments, who carried out raids on the important communication lines in the country, on mining centres, and on a whole host of strategic enemy-held installations and garrisons.

With ever-growing success came a torrent of volunteers so that, by the end of 1942, divisions and corps were formed. As pockets of liberated territory expanded, the scope of the national liberation war widened in various parts of Yugoslavia: Serbia, Bosnia, Croatia, Montenegro, Herzegovina, Slovenia and Macedonia.

In these freed areas, workshops were set up for making and repairing weapons, and at Užice an arms factory was operated. Besides repairing 4,500 rifles and some 600 machine-guns, this factory turned out 16,500 rifles, 2,700,000 bullets, 300 grenade-dischargers and 10,000 grenades in the October and November of 1941.

For four years, until the end of the war, the Yugoslav Liberation Army and Partisan Detachments carried on a continuous battle against the occupying forces, tying down many German and other divisions which would otherwise have been drafted to the Eastern or Western Fronts. There were, for instance, 37 enemy divisions in Yugoslavia by the middle of 1943. This was a war fought by the people of Yugoslavia in specific conditions, in which the National Liberation Army and Partisan Detachments grew step by step in a well-organised force. The struggle in Yugoslavia, therefore, contributed in large measure to the successes of the Allied powers in other theatres of war, besides driving enemy troops from Yugoslav soil.

Gradually, the areas wrested from the forces of occupation grew in size. Time after time, the Germans and their allies mounted large-scale offensives against the Army of Liberation, only to be beaten back in protracted battles during which bitter fighting took place. Casualties mounted; by the end of the war, the Yugoslav Liberation Army and Partisan Detachments had suffered a total of 305,000 killed and 425,000 injured soldiers and officers. Even higher were losses of the civilian population: more than 1,700,000 Yugoslavs were killed. Their enemies only lost 450,000 killed.

The National Liberation Army grew from a large number of small partisan groups, active all over the country, into a great national army, organ-

ised in armies, corps and divisions to the tune of 800,000 soldiers.

By the termination of hostilities in May, 1945, the Yugoslav Army, as the National Liberation Army was renamed, had succeeded in freeing the entire country from enemy domination, a truly notable achievement which clearly demonstrates the immense contribution to final victory made by the people of Yugoslavia.

THE WAR IN THE FAR EAST

Until December, 1941, the United States of America was neutral, although she showed a benevolent neutrality towards the Allies. It was all changed on the morning of Sunday, December 7th when, without warning, 360 aircraft from six Japanese aircraft-carriers suddenly attacked the American Pacific Fleet in Pearl Harbor, in the Hawaiian Islands. In an hour and forty minutes it was over; four great battleships were destroyed, four more were put out of action, and nearly every one of the 94 ships of war were damaged or sunk. Three days later the British battleships *Prince of Wales* and *Repulse* were sunk by Japanese aircraft off Malaya. Japan had shown her intention of dominating the Far East and had swiftly destroyed the principal naval opposition.

America joined the Allies, and Japan completed the Rome – Berlin – Tokyo Axis. The war was now world-wide indeed. For the next four years, men fought in the jungles and swamps of Malaya and Burma, on beaches of beautiful Pacific islands, in the Philippines and New Guinea, in the Solomon Islands and every part of the great area between Japan, Australia and eastern Asia. At first Japan met with success everywhere. She had made thorough preparations, established mastery in the air and on the sea, and she had internal supply routes. Japan took the Philippines from America and swiftly wrested Malaya and Burma from the British, until she stood on the threshold of Australia and at the very gates of India.

JAPAN'S TIDE OF SUCCESS

A few days after Pearl Harbor, strong Japanese forces were landed on Luzon, in the north of the Philippines, the main American base in the Pacific. It was a well-planned invasion, made at a number of points, and the attacks all converged on the capital, Manila. General MacArthur, the American commander, skilfully withdrew his forces to the Bataan Peninsula and Corregidor Island, there to stand at bay. The Americans were isolated from any help and the outcome was inevitable. Nevertheless, a grim fight followed which lasted five months. Sickness and disease took a heavier toll of both armies than did the actual battle. Bataan was forced to surrender early in April, 1942, and when the Japanese fought their way on to Corregidor in early May, that too was lost.

Malaya was also invaded in December, 1941, the Japanese making landings on the north-east coast. Malaya was defended by British and Indian troops, who had not completed the building of defensive positions in the north when the attacks were made. For a month the British and Indian units fought a rearguard action down the west coast of Malaya. It was a perplexing campaign; the Japanese were splendid jungle fighters and, whilst they could move noiselessly, they attacked with terrifying noise—shouting, screaming and using loud rattles to add to the din of machine-gun fire, and the explosions of mortar bombs and grenades.

It was a grim campaign, with the jungle full of its own strange noises, which might at any moment materialise into a fanatical attack by the Japanese. The enemy were constantly penetrating the jungle to appear behind the front line. Heavily outnumbered, and battle-weary, the British and Indian troops fell back southwards to Singapore, the great naval fortress on the southern tip of Malaya.

The survivors reached Singapore in February, 1942, and were soon plunged into the last round of the battle for Malaya. As the fortress had been built to withstand attack from the sea, defences and guns were all directed southwards—but the Japanese columns were advancing from the north. The island of Singapore is separated from the mainland by a strait, which varies between 600 and 2,000 yards in width, and the causeway which bridged the strait had been demolished. On February 8th the Japanese assault began, and only seven days later Singapore was forced to surrender. The 70,000 soldiers on the island became prisoners of war, and Malaya was entirely in Japanese hands.

121. The first wave of U. S. troops to land on Saipan beach, in the Marianas, use a sand-dune as cover from enemy fire.

122. Grim-faced and weary, American troops press on after 19 days of continuous action.

121

123

122

124

125

23. A jungle battle-headquarters during the operations on Guadalcanal.

24. From foxhole to foxhole, U.S. troops move steadily on across Iwo Jima.

25. Under withering Japanese fire, American troops lie low behind a coconut-log barricade in Tarawa.

It was the same everywhere in the Pacific. Java and Sumatra fell, and the Japanese invaded Burma, north of Malaya. This was, perhaps, the most dangerous threat of all, for Burma leads to East Pakistan and India. The British, Indian and Commonwealth army in Burma was without sea communications and heavily outnumbered. The troops made an epic retreat northwards, fighting off their pursuers whenever possible, and falling back until they stood at bay on an 800-mile front north from Akyab through Imphal, guarding the gateway to India.

THE TIDE TURNS IN THE PACIFIC

During 1942 and 1943, Britain, Australia, New Zealand, India and America prepared for the gigantic counter-attack which would be necessary to liberate Japanese-occupied territory and bring about Japan's final defeat. Warships and aircraft-carriers were built, assault craft were constructed in hundreds, and men were trained to cope with the special problems of jungle warfare. Carefully integrated plans were made, and troops and materials were moved into position.

In December, 1944, the British Commonwealth Fourteenth Army, based on India, which had been guarding the country against Japanese attacks, itself went over to the attack. The Fourteenth Army made a double advance: one southwards down the west coast of Burma towards Rangoon, and the other across the River Chindwin towards Mandalay. As strong air support was available, gliders and parachute-drops were employed to maintain the advancing army with men and supplies.

The soldiers fought in "jungle green" and, for better camouflage, nets over their steel helmets were dressed with twigs. The men knew how to hack their way through thick jungle, and they had learned the tricks of hard-living, and of swift and silent movement. The Japanese fought with fanatical courage, often to the last man, but now the skill and material advantage were on the other side. The Fourteenth Army could not be stopped. Mandalay was recaptured on March 20th, 1945, and then, swinging southwards, the divisions hastened to aid the advance on Rangoon, which was taken on May 3rd. Thus Burma was cleared of the Japanese.

The Americans went into action at the same time in a number of places, as part of a concerted plan to oust the Japanese from their newly-conquered empire and drive them back to their own country. A memorable landing was made in April, 1945, by United States Marines on the island of Okinawa, between Formosa and Japan. This vital and strongly-held base was taken only after ten weeks of furious fighting in which the Japanese losses amounted to 100,000 killed.

The tide had turned to the full and, during the spring and early summer of 1945, the Japanese, always fighting with scorn for death, were overcome on every front. The Allies were poised for the invasion of Japan.

At this stage of the war, an historic event occurred which was to have far-reaching effects on war and weapons, and which, like the invention of gunpowder, changed the role and function of soldiers. A specific warning was sent to Japan on July 26th, 1945. It was rejected and, on August 5th, an atomic bomb was dropped on the Japanese city of Hiroshima. The single bomb was more destructive than 20,000 tons of T.N.T., and more than half the city of twelve square miles was utterly demolished.

The Japanese Government still refused to surrender so, on August 9th, a second atomic bomb was dropped, on Nagasaki, with the same terrible result. On August 10th, Japan asked for terms and, four days later, her unconditional surrender was accepted by the Allies. The war was over, and the world had entered the Atomic Age.

COMMANDOS
AND SPECIAL
SERVICE TROOPS

126

127

The word *Commando* came into general use as a result of the South African War of 1899–1902. A commando was an administrative and tactical unit in the Boer Army, consisting of men from one district. Commandos often fought as small independent units, making raids on British columns.

In the modern sense, commandos are specially picked and trained soldiers who perform difficult and usually hazardous tasks. They may raid an enemy headquarters behind the lines, or destroy a vital bridge or important objective, and they prepare the way for an assault invasion. Sometimes they reach their objective by parachute, sometimes they steal up to an enemy-held beach in canoes launched from submarines.

Commandos are adventurous volunteers selected for their toughness, self-reliance, initiative and steady nerves. They can climb steep cliffs, find their way through hostile country, survive under the most difficult conditions and, when necessary, act very quickly. They handle explosives, and their weapons are usually the hand-grenade, the knife or bare hands.

The commando is the descendant of the heroes of the "Forlorn Hopes" of the past. Their predecessors led the way through the breaches of besieged cities, and up the cliff-path to the Heights of Abraham when General Wolfe captured Quebec in 1759, and so won Canada.

26. You have to be tough in the Commandos. This Sergeant clings expertly to the cliff face, 00 ft above the sea.

27. Final inspection before a party of 'Red Berets' — the world-famous British airborne troops — emplane on an overseas mission.

28. Mussolini on his release from captivity by German parachutists.

29. Popski's Private Army. Lt.–Col. V. Penikoff, founder-leader of the unique long-range desert group, in his armed jeep.

THE RAID OF ST NAZAIRE

World War II provided a wide range of tasks for commandos and other special service units. A famous operation was the raid on the French harbour of St Nazaire in March, 1942. The German battleship *Tirpitz* was lying in Trondheim fjord, Norway, and if she put to sea to attack Allied convoys, the only dock large enough to take her was St Nazaire. If, therefore, that dock were to be destroyed, there was less chance of the *Tirpitz* putting to sea. The objective of the raid was to penetrate the strong defences of St Nazaire and destroy the gates of the great lock.

A convoy of destroyers and light naval craft sailed from Falmouth, carrying 250 commandos. With them sailed the *Campbeltown*, an old destroyer carrying three tons of high explosive in her bows. The convoy approached St Nazaire and the *Campbeltown* rammed the dock gates, under intense and murderous fire. While the fuses were being set, the commandos leaped ashore to destroy the dock machinery. Furious fighting developed with the German troops defending the port. In a short time, some of the tasks of damaging the docks were achieved but, overwhelmed by numbers, all but five of the landing party were killed or captured. Four of the commandos received the Victoria Cross. The *Campbeltown* did not blow up then but, next day, while a party of senior German officers was inspecting the wreck of the ship jammed in the lock gates, she blew up, killing hundreds of Germans and putting the dock out of action for the rest of the war.

THE RESCUE OF MUSSOLINI

When Mussolini's government collapsed in July, 1943, he was interned and taken to a small mountain resort in central Italy, where he was guarded by several hundred Italian Carabinieri. Then, one night in the September, Berlin radio announced the startling news that Mussolini had been "liberated" from the former hotel in which he had been held prisoner. According to the bulletin, the rescue was carried out as follows.

Perched on the 9,000-foot mountain of Gran Sasso, in the Abruzzi

Mountains, the hotel was raided by a group of German parachutists, who were dropped from a plane and came down only a few hundred feet above the building. Speedily, the special airborne troops took up their positions and, as reinforcements arrived, the S.S. leader of the rescue party climbed over a ten-foot wall to reach the hotel's main entrance.

This was heavily guarded by carabinieri, armed with machine-guns. Pointing his pistol at the Italians, the S.S. leader ordered them to put up their hands—and they immediately obeyed. Catching sight of Mussolini at a window, the S.S. leader stormed into the hotel at the head of his men, and found the ex-dictator in the custody of two police officials.

Berlin's report of this special military operation continued with a description of the scene which followed.

"Duce, the Führer sends me to liberate you!" exclaimed the German officer. Embracing him, Mussolini replied: "I guessed it. I never doubted the Führer would do everything to get me out."

By the time Mussolini and his liberators emerged from the building, a Fieseler Storch aircraft was waiting outside on the plateau, to fly the fallen dictator away to German-held territory.

SPECIAL SERVICE UNITS

Special service units came into being during World War II for operating in many different ways. In the Western Desert the British Long Range Desert Group, and "Popski's Private Army", commanded by Lieutenant-Colonel Peniakoff, operated far behind the enemy's lines. They would drive off into the desert in small groups of jeeps or trucks and disappear for weeks. Navigating by sextant and compass they would make their way to vital positions far behind the enemy's front and go into action.

In Europe, dangerous and lonely missions were performed by specially

130. Helicopter-borne American troops.

131. Paratroopers leap from their aircraft i rapid succession.

132. This American motor-bike trooper tore into position at 35 m. p. h., and was in action within three seconds.

133. Nowadays, whole divisions are speedily transported halfway across the world by air.

trained men or women who were dropped by parachute, or landed by plane at night, to organise and work with the Resistance. From Italy, special service troops sailed in small fishing boats, loaded with supplies and ammunition, to land secretly on German-occupied Greek islands. There they would go into hiding until they could raid the headquarters.

Commandos were used in combined operations, in Sicily, Salerno and Normandy. During the early planning stages, they would examine the selected landing beaches to make charts and plans. A few hours before the actual invasion, commandos were dropped by parachute to destroy machine-gun nests and strongpoints, clearing the way for the main assault.

PARACHUTE TROOPS

The Germans used parachute troops in their early campaigns, and they would have been used in large numbers if Hitler had ordered the invasion of Britain in 1940. But the first full-scale use of airborne troops was on Crete in May, 1941. After the fall of Greece, most of the British and New Zealand troops which had gone to her aid withdrew to Crete. There, the German Army and Air Force combined in a new form of attack.

The initial assault was made against Malene airfield in Crete, a heavily defended position. Eight battalions of German parachutists were dropped, and although nearly all were killed at once, they continued to come. The German Parachute Division was the *Corps d'élite*, and the young, highly trained and dedicated Nazis gloried in their opportunity. Five thousand parachutists were dropped near the airfield on the first day; the attack was supported by gliders, which crash-landed to disgorge more troops. After three days, the airfield was in German hands, and then troop-carrying planes poured in; scores were shot down, but always more arrived. In ten days, Crete was entirely in German hands.

The same method was used by the Allies when their turn came. In 1945, on one day, troops of the First Allied Airborne Army landed in Holland, the British 1st Airborne Division landed at Arnhem, and two American Airborne Divisions landed at Nijmegen and at Eindhoven.

Airborne operations had an important part in the campaigns in the Far East. Entire units, fully equipped and armed, were landed in the jungle behind the enemy's lines, on temporary airfields made by parachutists. Wingate's famous Chindits operated deep in central Burma, entirely supplied by air. These specially trained brigades were fully equipped for their role. Commanded by Major-General Orde Wingate, they were flown far into the jungle, where parachutists cleared the dense undergrowth to make landing grounds for the reception of reinforcements and equipment.

The modern tendency is for large and composite Air Assault divisions. These experimental formations may consist of an air assault infantry battalion, a composite artillery battalion, an aviation group, an air cavalry troop, and an air support group. Such divisions could operate as follows: the air cavalry, in helicopters, hold the enemy while the infantry, also in helicopters, are put down, supported by the air artillery in helicopters and low-flying rocket-firing aircraft.

Special Service troops are available for every kind of operation as, for example, the Frogmen, who are specialists in underwater attacks with explosives on ships and installations. Once soldiers had to march to find the enemy; now they can strike swiftly wherever he is. The British Army has the Parachute Regiment, which wears a red beret; the Special Air Service, with a beige beret; and the Army Air Corps, which operates light aircraft for reconnaissance and liaison work, with a light blue beret. Their job of piloting army transport aircraft is now to be handed over to the Royal Corps of Transport, formerly known as the R.A.S.C.

134. A canoeist Commando hands a limpet-mine to his frogman companion.

135. Training frogmen in the technique of boarding a moving vessel.

GUNS AND GUNNERS

136. Heavy howitzer being fired in France during 1916.

137. French artillery pictured in action at St Quentin, 1918.

138. New Zealand gunners manning a field gun during the First World War.

Cannon had become reasonably accurate by the eighteenth century and artillerymen were proud of their guns and of their skill. Infantry battalions usually had two light three- or six-pounders with one officer, two non-commissioned officers and twelve men to serve them. Full batteries of heavier guns were used to engage and cover vital points in battle, or to bombard infantry before an attack. They were also used to batter the walls of a besieged town or fortress, to dislodge the masonry and make breaches for the assault. Horse artillery became as dashing and as colourful as the light cavalry, the men splendidly uniformed and plumed, horses and guns beautifully groomed and polished. They would gallop into position at speed, unhitch the horses, unlimber the guns and swing them into action. Range was short, and the fighting often took place at close quarters. There are many stirring tales of gunners fighting to the death to save their guns from capture, for, to the artilleryman, his guns are what the Colours are to the infantry.

In those days, guns were muzzle-loaders, and the ammunition was cannon-balls or primitive fused gunpowder shells. The invention of the breech-loading gun and the introduction of high-explosive shells revolutionised gunnery in the nineteenth century. Increasingly powerful charges of high explosive and improved mechanism increased the range until gunners eventually aimed at targets they could not see. They were controlled by a forward Observation Officer who gave the range by signal, first with flags, then by field telephone and finally by radio. In World War I, observation was sometimes made from captive balloons and aeroplanes.

ARTILLERY IN WORLD WAR I

Artillery methods made considerable advances between 1914 and 1918. The regular bombardment of enemy trenches and troop concentrations became a routine. The Germans used particularly heavy guns with immense range. Shrapnel came into general use; the shells were fused to explode above the heads of the enemy, and these made steel helmets essential. Gas shells were used by both sides after the Germans had introduced poison gas in the Battle of Ypres, in 1915. Massed guns were used to prepare for an infantry attack, followed by a barrage of fire which moved ahead of the advancing infantry.

The increasing use of aircraft brought into being the anti-aircraft gun and, simultaneously, the searchlight battery, which was first operated in the British Army by the Royal Engineers. A smaller type of artillery was the trench mortar, used by the infantry to lob bombs into enemy trenches. In World War I, artillery fell into three main divisions: heavy or garrison artillery; howitzers for firing with high elevation; and light or field artillery.

ARTILLERY IN WORLD WAR II

World War II saw further changes in weapons. Part of the thunder of the gunners was stolen by the airmen. Massed bombing attacks could wreak terrible havoc on targets far out of range of guns, and low-flying dive-bombing attacks on infantry were often more telling than any artillery fire. But the gunners still played a vital part in battle.

At the Battle of El Alamein, on October 23rd, 1942, for example, nearly a thousand guns of the British Eighth Army opened fire precisely at 9.40 p.m. For twenty minutes, until Zero Hour for the infantry, they fired unceasingly on the German and Italian gun positions. Exactly at 10.0 p.m., when the infantry began to advance, the range was shortened to shell the enemy forward defensive positions.

A development born of the wider use of the tank was the self-propelled gun, a heavy gun mounted on a tank chassis, able to make its own way over rough ground. Anti-aircraft guns were of great importance in a war in which heavy air attack featured so largely. British and American bombers on raids over Europe had to run the gauntlet of intense anti-aircraft fire, and Britain was dotted with anti-aircraft sites. New guns were developed to reach high-flying aircraft, and coloured tracer shells were employed to assist the gunners.

In the history of war, a new weapon has always produced a reply. The tank was invented to overcome the stalemate of trench, wire and machine-gun. The answer to the tank was the anti-tank gun. As the armament of tanks was increased, so was the power of the anti-tank gun. Light anti-tank guns were used by the infantry for fighting tanks at close range, and heavier anti-tank guns were used by the artillery. World War II saw artillery divided into three main types: field; anti-tank; and anti-aircraft.

GUIDED MISSILES

Muzzle-loaders firing cannon-balls were succeeded by breech-loaders firing high-explosive shells. These, in their turn, have been surpassed in range, efficiency and deadliness by the guided missile. The gun has become merely a launching device, while the missile itself provides its own propulsion and is directed to its target in flight.

Heavier missiles, such as ground-to-air weapons, are enormous shells packed with complicated electronic devices behind a powerful war-head, with rockets attached. The rockets provide the propulsion, while the electronic and gyroscopic devices in the missile guide it to the target. The missile travels cradled on a large truck, accompanied by its radar apparatus

139

139. An Italian 105 mm. Pack howitzer operated by British troops in Aden, 1962.

140. The Big Sebastopol Gun 'Schwerer Gustav' mounted on double railtracks.

141. Giant rocket on parade in Moscow.

142. A French guided-missile is fired by hovering American helicopter.

and a truck containing the control apparatus. These convoys of tremendously powerful, and tremendously costly, weapons are a far cry from the jingling and jaunty Horse Artillery of fifty years ago.

Guided missiles have also been developed for use against tanks. These are front-line weapons which can be carried by one man, and can be brought quickly into action against tanks at a range of from two hundred yards to a mile. When fired, they are guided during flight by a hand-held control. Pressure on a trigger sends electrical signals along a wire fed from the rear of the missile. The missile contains gyroscopic devices behind the war-head, and a rocket motor; steering is by electronic devices. The war-head explodes on contact with the target, and is capable of piercing the thickest armour-plate.

143. Symbolising the artillery of today, a sentinel rocket on its launching-pad is silhouetted against the sky.

144. Speeding towards its test-target, a Thunderbird roars upward over the Irish Sea.

143

144

MILITARY ENGINEERS

The engineers enable an army to live, to move and to fight. Generally speaking, in an attack they are the first in, and in a retreat the last out. Armies have always had their engineers—the specialists and experts with the necessary skills to support and aid the fighting men. King Henry V had his engineers at Agincourt, in 1415. The unit was commanded by Sir John Greyndon and contained: 120 miners; Thomas Matthew and William Temple, both Master Carpenters, with 124 carpenters under them; John Bennet, a Master Mason, with 120 labourers; Richard Hodel and Thomas Smith, with 12 yeoman smiths. That list is typical of an engineer unit—miners first, and then craftsmen for special tasks.

Three hundred years later, the records of the Train of Engineers on one of the Duke of Marlborough's campaigns included, among others, a Company of Bridgemen, a Captain of the Tin Boats, a Lieutenant of the Boats,

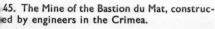
45. The Mine of the Bastion du Mat, construc-ted by engineers in the Crimea.
45

a Master Cooper with his men, and a Master Basket-maker.

DIVERSITY OF SKILLS

The duties of the engineers in an army have always been diverse; they are there to do anything the commander requires, and it is their pride never to fail. As warfare became more complicated, so the variety of the engineers' tasks increased. Modern military engineers can construct roads, bridges, buildings and docks. They can also destroy them with explosives, to delay the enemy. They can operate ports, or inland waterways. They make maps, operate electricity generators, provide electricity systems, lay pipe-lines, and organise the postal service of an army. Until 1922, the British Corps of Royal Engineers was responsible for communications and signals, with flag, carrier pigeon, field telephone or dispatch rider, until R. E. Signals became the Royal Corps of Signals. Currently, they are handing over responsibility for military railways to the R.A.S.C. (which is being renamed the Royal Corps of Transport), and their supply functions to the R.A.O.C.

SAPPERS AND MINERS

Mining was one of the earliest tasks of the engineers. They dug saps, or trenches, obliquely towards a besieged fortress, and dug the sites for the siege-guns. When the walls were breached, it was usually an officer of Engineers who had the honour of leading the storming party. Because of their ancient skill in digging saps, the engineers of the British Army are known as Sappers.

The Sappers and Miners of the day cut the galleries in the Rock of Gibraltar before the siege of 1779, and they dug and constructed Wellington's Lines of Torres Vedras in Portugal in 1810.

146. Modern anti-mine pneumatic boots lessen the danger to the sweeper.

147. The Ack Pack flame-thrower is used to clear dense undergrowth as an aid to detection of hidden mines.

148. Bomb disposal is an important task of engineers, particularly in wartime.

COLOUR PLATES

TOP: American and Danish troops taking part in a joint parade.

BOTTOM: Lapp and Norwegian troops.

ABOVE: Troops of the French Foreign Legion on parade with their armoured vehicles.

BELOW: Italian guardsman at the Tomb of the Unknown Warrior in Rome.

TOP RIGHT: Cadets on parade at West Point, America's military academy.

BOTTOM RIGHT: Evzones on guard at the Royal Palace in Athens.

TOP. This Class 40 Floating Bailey Bridge was erected across the Seine in 1944.

BOTTOM. During manoeuvres in 1962, the Sappers built this Light Assault Floating Bridge over the Weser near Sweringen.

COLOUR PLATE

TOP: Republic Day parade in Delhi, showing Indian camel corps troops.

BOTTOM: Mounted bodyguard of the President of Pakistan.

There was a great deal of mining in World War I, when engineers of both sides tunnelled under the enemy trenches to build large chambers for explosive charges. Sometimes the tunnelling was detected, and then the opposing engineers would dig their tunnel to meet the enemy. Fierce battles were fought deep underground with pistols and shovels. Engineers erected the defensive wire systems in front of trenches, and repaired them, working out in No-man's-land, where a clumsy move or sound could be followed by the glare of a Very light and then deadly machine-gun fire.

MINING AND MINE DETECTING

Use of the tank in World War II brought the anti-tank mine into being, and this was the responsibility of the engineers. They laid the mines, buried under the ground and fused so that they would explode when a tank touched them, and they cleared enemy mines. This was done with a mine-detector sweeping the ground, until mines were made so that they could not be so detected. Then the Sappers had to find them by prodding the ground. When uncovered, the fuse was removed. The Sappers lead an attack, clearing and marking a path through the enemy minefield.

The Engineers also provided highly-skilled Bomb Disposal Units to deal with unexploded bombs after an air raid. It was a task requiring expert skill and very steady nerves. When the bomb was located, it was exposed, and then made safe by the removal of the fuses—an extremely dangerous task. This was made even more terrifying when the bomb was fitted with a time-fuse which could be heard ticking away as the expert worked on it.

FOSTER-PARENTS TO NEW IDEAS

It has long been the custom for the Army to entrust new ideas to the

engineers to be developed, for they are by nature ingenious and enterprising. We have seen that the Royal Engineers were partly responsible for the invention of the tank, and they took over the first motor transport for the Army. They developed and operated searchlights, until coastal searchlights were taken over by the Royal Navy and the anti-aircraft searchlights by the Royal Artillery.

One new baby entrusted to the Royal Engineers was submarine mining. A unit of Submarine Miners, R.E., was formed in 1871 to organise and operate underwater mines for the defence of British ports. The Royal Engineers were not new to the subject, for over the previous fifty years they had developed a successful technique for blowing up sunken wrecks.

The underwater defences made great progress and further units were formed, while work was also done on the torpedo. This was so successful that, by 1885, an underwater guided missile, the Brennan torpedo, had been tested and proved; it had a speed of 25 knots, a range of more than 1,000 yards, and its course was controlled by the firer. In 1905, underwater defence by sea-mining, and the torpedo as a weapon, were taken over by the Royal Navy.

BALLOONS, AIRSHIPS AND AEROPLANES

Military flying was another foster-child of the Royal Engineers. It began in 1878 with captive balloons for enemy observation and, ten years later, captive balloons were used on active service in Bechuanaland. In the South African War, three Balloon Sections were in operation. Another method, and rather a hair-raising one, was to use kites. A string of kites was flown and, when it was considered enough lift had been obtained, a basket was hitched to the line, a man got in, and up he went.

153

152. Flexible road trackway can be laid at the rate of 55 yards in eleven seconds by this 3-ton Bedford truck.

153. Sappers at work on an air-conditioner unit being installed at a military camp in Aden.

When the internal combustion engine became available as a power unit, the Sappers built and flew airships. One of the most famous was the *Nulli Secundus*, which made a three-and-a-half hour flight from Farnborough to London in 1907, circling the dome of St Paul's Cathedral. Airships were much used in World War I, especially by the Germans, whose famous Zeppelins made the first air raids on London.

When the Wright brothers flew the first powered aeroplane in America in 1903, every country saw the military value of flying. The first British Army aeroplane was the Cody biplane, which was flown successfully in 1910. The Royal Engineers, basically diggers in the ground, took to the air, and an Air Battalion was formed in 1911 to operate all the Army's balloons, airships and aeroplanes. A year later this responsibility was taken over by the newly-formed Royal Flying Corps, which later became the Royal Air Force.

The modern military engineers bring their traditional ingenuity and know-how to the complicated methods of modern war. They are assisted by modern equipment, such as large bulldozers and levellers, they have their specially modified tanks and, like every modern soldier, they are highly mechanised. Bridging has always been an important aspect of their work. The Bailey Bridge, invented by a British Sapper officer, brilliantly solved the bridging problems of World War II. Since 1945, it has been used extensively for civilian purposes when emergencies or repairs put the ordinary bridge out of action.

Engineers are dropped by parachute on special operations, they take part in commando raids to destroy vital installations, and they go ashore with the first flight in a combined operation. Their pride is that they can do anything, anywhere, to help the army to live, to move and to fight.

THE MEN
BEHIND
THE LINE

The armoured troops, infantry and artillery are the teeth and claws of an army; but more than teeth and claws are required. For every man in the line, there must be eight or nine behind the line to keep him there. The fighting man has to be fed, his weapons have to be supplied with ammunition and his vehicles replenished with fuel, and for these and many other essential services a large and intricate organisation is necessary.

FOOD AND FUEL

In the old days, armies lived on the land, taking their food where they could find it. They fared handsomely with conquest, poorly at other times. Some armies, including the British, had their main rations supplied. These were either brought forward from base depots, or purchased from civilians in the area where the army was campaigning. The Duke of Wellington said that he always liked to be able to trace a biscuit from its factory in England to the soldier's mouth, for he realised that happy soldiers are well-fed soldiers.

154

The custom then was for men to form messes of three, taking it in turn to cook over a camp fire. One man from each mess would parade for the meat issue, all standing with their backs to the meat and choosing a piece without looking, to make it fair. The meat, nearly always salted mutton, was stewed with whatever extras were available—perhaps rice, duff or potatoes. Sometimes there was no meat, and the hard-baked biscuits were stewed instead to make a kind of porridge.

Soldiers' rations have steadily improved over the past hundred years, especially with the invention of tinned food, and now great care is taken to provide soldiers with three good meals a day, appetising and varied. The catering for an army of perhaps 200,000 men is a vast problem. Anyone who has had to buy the food for a camping party of twenty for a week will appreciate the immensity of the problem involved in feeding an army. There must be enough, without any waste, and the many items required to provide three good meals a day make the problem gigantic.

The quantity is only half the problem; it must be delivered at the right place, at the right time, in good condition. The rations must be delivered at the base depot, a port or a railhead, and then distributed to depots and sub-depots, so that they can be delivered to every unit. Sometimes on active service the last link is to an outlying unit which can only be reached by mules up a narrow mountain path, or by dropping the food supplies from the air. Ration lorries and ration parties are an obvious target for the enemy; whatever the difficulties, however, the rations must get through.

Base and field bakeries make bread, and cooks are trained to take charge of unit cook-houses. During operations men carry forty-eight hour rations in their haversacks, and emergency rations for a further twenty-four hours;

155

54. Horse transport moving over a stretch
f rough country.

55. The training of Army bakers in progress.

but normal rations are always got through to fighting troops as soon as possible, sometimes taken forward ready-cooked, in insulated containers.

During World War II, a fourteen-day pack was introduced. Consisting of a case containing everything one man required for fourteen days, these packs have the added advantage of being equally efficient at feeding fourteen men for one day, seven men for two days, and so on.

The supply of fuel to tanks and vehicles presents a similar problem; it must be delivered at the right place and at the right time, or tracks and wheels are brought to a standstill. The same method of distribution is used.

In the British Army, the supply of rations and fuel has until now been the responsibility of the Royal Army Service Corps, which was the first of its kind in any army of the world. Reorganisation has accompanied the Corps's latest change of name, from R.A.S.C. to Royal Corps of Transport. In future, the supply of rations and fuel will be undertaken by the R.A.O.C. The Royal Corps of Transport has developed from the ancient Commissaries of Muster, becoming in turn the Royal Wagon Train, the Land Transport Corps, the Military Train, the Commissariat and Transport Corps, and then The Army Service Corps, or popularly "Ally Sloper's Cavalry". The prefix "Royal" was awarded after World War I.

The development of special supply corps came with the realisation that the success of a campaign depended on the efficiency of the supply and transport services. Such troops, whatever their designation, are responsible for supplying an army with its rations and fuel, and it is their pride that they always get the supplies through, no matter what the difficulties. Service troops provide transport and drivers; sometimes, in wild terrain, they have to employ mule-trains. The British service corps has also manned small ships when necessary, although this duty may now be transferred to the Royal Navy. During the Italian campaign in World War II, Greek

156

157

158

and Yugoslav fishing boats which plied between British-held territory and German-occupied Greek islands were commanded by an R.A.S.C. sergeant, with two or three privates as crew.

R.A.S.C. soldiers were originally experts with horses, upon which they relied for military haulage. Later, they became expert drivers of motor trucks. Now they work with aircraft, exercising their traditional expertise loading supplies into freighters and air-transport planes.

World War II gave many examples of the problems of supply, and in some cases of the disaster which follows failure. The German armies fighting on the Eastern front were far from home, and the long, attenuated supply routes across Poland and western Russia were highly vulnerable to attack, a fact of which the Russians took every advantage. The problem became intensified when the harsh Russian winter closed down on them, and the result was virtually a repetition of the grim disaster which befell Napoleon's army one hundred and thirty years earlier.

AMMUNITION AND WEAPONS

Fighting men must be supplied with ammunition, weapons and equipment, and skilled and fully equipped craftsmen must be readily available to maitain, repair and replace guns, tanks and vehicles.

The organisation necessary to keep an army supplied with these essentials is intricate, and needs a lot of experts. There are many kinds of ammunition: bullets for rifles, automatic rifles and machine-guns; shells of all kinds for the artillery and tanks; mortar bombs, grenades, mines and explosives. All these have to be stored correctly and safely, and in such a way that any ammunition required can be delivered swiftly.

An army needs a wide range of equipment: radio sets and field telephones; range-finders; such items as binoculars and compasses. Sufficient must be available at all times, and everything must be carefully stored and looked after. Ammunition, weapons and equipment are the ordnance stores, and in the British Army they are the responsibility of the Royal Army Ordnance Corps. The Corps of Royal Mechanical and Electrical Engineers, or R.E.M.E., inspects, maintains, modifies and repairs the army's machinery and technical equipment.

A GREAT DIVERSITY OF SERVICES

The examples given above are only some of the essential services behind the fighting line, which every modern army has to have, even though the precise manner in which they are organised varies slightly from country to country. In Britain, the Royal Corps of Signals, which was originally part of the Royal Engineers, manages communications within an army by radio, telephone, or dispatch rider. The Intelligence Corps collects, collates and interprets information, questions prisoners, and is trained in such tasks as interpreting aerial photographs—all so that a commander may be provided with accurate information about the enemy.

The health of an army and, in battle, the care of the wounded, requires a large organisation of doctors, nurses and orderlies, and field or base hospital accommodation. Ambulance drivers and stretcher-bearers are also required. Traditionally, in the British Army, regimental bandsmen become stretcher-bearers in battle, and there are many occasions when they have won awards for bringing back wounded soldiers under fire.

A small corps, formerly large and important, looks after animals. Veterinary surgeons and their staffs serve for this purpose, and they are

56. A scout-car is repaired under fire.

57. The maintenance of a truck by soldiers of the King's African Rifles is supervised by a R.E.M.E. mechanic.

58. A blood transfusion being given to an American stretcher-case in Sicily during the Second World War.

159. Chaplains work closely with medical units in the field.

160. A signalman seen at work on overhead telegraph lines.

still required when mules are used for transport in mountainous country, or where a camel corps is employed. Yet another branch of medicine has its place in the modern army: dentists serve in order to attend to the soldiers' teeth. Perfect health is essential for full efficiency, and the dentist has his part to play in the complex organisation.

The spiritual well-being of troops, and many aspects of their welfare, is in the care of chaplains, often termed Padres. Chaplains of all the main denominations of an army are enrolled, and for them a battalion or regiment is their parish. The padre is the man to whom a soldier can turn if he is in personal trouble; he acts as confessor, adviser and family welfare officer—a hard-working settler of soldiers' problems.

An army needs its own police, or Provost Corps, distinguished in the American Army by white steel helmets and in the British Army by red tops to their caps. Military police control traffic, preserve order and provide guards for special establishments, sometimes with highly intelligent dogs.

It has become the custom to enable young soldiers to learn a trade or profession while serving in the army, so that, when they end their military career, they can obtain a good civilian job. This is catered for, in the British Army, by the Royal Army Education Corps. It is manned by officers and men qualified to teach, and lectures and lessons in a variety of subjects are arranged for units. During World War II, the R.A.E.C. lectured the troops on the background of the war, so that a soldier knew why he was serving and with what object.

Spiritual, medical and mental welfare having been provided for, the soldier's chief need lies in physical training. His physique is duly looked after by qualified instructors whose physical fitness and amazing ability, in and out of the gymnasium, ensures that the soldier of today has the stamina and endurance necessary to carry out the most exacting duties.

WOMEN IN THE ARMY

In times gone by, women always accompanied soldiers to war. The French Army had its *vivandières*, to provide an early kind of canteen service, to wash, mend and sew, and to care for the sick and wounded soldiers. A regiment of any nationality would be followed on the march by smart carriages bearing the officers' wives, whilst the women and children of the regiment rode on the baggage wagons. A regiment was a complete community, with the Colonel at its head, and the women and children as much members, and as fiercely proud of its good name, as the soldiers themselves.

The casualties in the old days were not limited to the soldiers, either. There is, for example, a memorial tablet at Secondèrabad to the 45th, or 1st Nottinghamshire Regiment, which reads: "Erected to the memory of those who have died from the date of embarkation to India, January, 1819, to November, 1836—22 officers, 70 sergeants, 44 corporals, 17

161. Florence Nightingale, 'The Lady with the Lamp', in the hospital at Scutari, during the Crimean War.

162. At the siege of Mafeking, Mrs Davis took her place in the trenches alongside the men.

161

162

drummers, 995 privates, 163 women, 183 children."

The modern army has its married quarters for women and children, and in peacetime a number of them accompany the regiment or corps overseas, but in wartime a regiment goes on active service without its families. Instead, women have established a place in the army in their own right, either as nurses or in a women's corps.

THE TRADITION OF FLORENCE NIGHTINGALE

Florence Nightingale landed at Scutari, in the Crimea, in 1854, with forty nurses, to the dismay of the older doctors and officers, who felt that it was unseemly for a woman, especially a well-born person like Miss Nightingale, to nurse rough soldiers.

But Florence Nightingale was a young woman of character and determination. She swept aside all opposition and took charge of the military hospital at Scutari. She burned the foul bedding, had the whole place cleaned and scrubbed, and issued a set of strict regulations. She and her nurses then began to care for the sick and wounded soldiers as they thought proper, with wonderful effect. The death rate began to fall immediately, and the "rough soldiers" became mild and obedient, worshipping "The Lady with the Lamp", as they called their saviour.

Florence Nightingale began a great tradition. After the Crimean War, nurses were installed in every military hospital; the British Nursing Service was formed, and this was copied by other countries. The nursing service was developed at the same time as the International Red Cross, which came from an idea of Swiss philanthropist Henri Dunant. In 1864, most countries subscribed to a convention for the humane treatment of the wounded and of prisoners of war. The convention was revised in 1906.

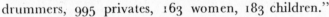

WOMEN'S CORPS

In modern armies, women also wear military uniforms and undertake a wide variety of tasks formerly only carried out by the men; in some they actually bear arms. The normal role of women soldiers, however, is to do work which releases men to serve in the fighting line. The British A.T.S. (Auxiliary Territorial Service), which in 1949 became the W.R.A.C. (Women's Royal Army Corps), has the same ranks, badges of rank and organisation as the rest of the Army.

Women soldiers drive lorries, staff-cars and ambulances; they are radio and telephone operators, and experts in electronic apparatus; they code and decode signals; they work as secretaries, typists, clerks and store-keepers. Expert caterers and cooks, women soldiers can also repair technical apparatus and, indeed, perform almost any necessary duty.

During World War II women served with the artillery on anti-aircraft sites, and were of the greatest value during the anxious months of the Battle of Britain. While the men fired the guns, the women operated radar for spotting enemy planes and handled the ammunition.

WOMEN IN THE FRONT LINE

In the Balkan kingdom of Serbia during World War I, Flora Sandes became the only British woman in the fighting ranks of any Allied Army.

After spending the early part of the war helping the Serbian Red Cross, both as a nurse and as leader of a campaign to raise money for the purchase of medical supplies, Flora Sandes joined Serbia's "Iron Regiment" as a private, and remained with it throughout the duration of hostilities.

Promotion to corporal and then sergeant followed, and she took part in fighting with the Serbian Army at Salonika in 1916.

Flora Sandes was treated in the same way as every other Serbian soldier, except that she carried a carbine instead of a rifle and, as a sergeant, was allotted a batman.

When in action, this amazing woman carried no equipment beyond her carbine, a 65-round cartridge belt, revolver, water-bottle, overcoat, light canvas ground-sheet, and a steel helmet. She experienced a spell of one month when her regiment was actually fighting non-stop, day and night.

Wounded in 1916, by a hand-grenade which exploded on contact with the revolver in her holster, Flora Sandes rejoined the regiment six months later, and played her full part in all the horrors, perils and trials of trench warfare. Sergeant Sandes proved herself the equal of any man, and led her troops with great bravery and distinction—so much so that, after the armistice in 1918, she remained on in the Serbian Army.

A year later, by special Act of Parliament, Flora Sandes was promoted to commissioned rank. Demobbed in 1922, she was retained on the reserve and, in that capacity, received further promotion, to captain, in 1926.

There are numerous examples of women taking an active part in war during the years which followed the achievements of Flora Sandes.

They have fought skilfully with rifles and machine-guns alongside the men. They served in the Spanish Civil War with the Republicans, and many of the bands of partisans who lived in the mountains of central Europe had women serving with them, women who shared the rough life and fought with the men. In Israel, women have a special place as fighting troops.

Soldiering is generally a man's calling, but women have proved that when necessary they can play a man's part, and play it well.

63. Women made a valuable contribution to the war-effort in military stores such as this.

64. Czech woman sniper Maria Lalkova in action on the Russian front during the Second World War.

65. Weapon-cleaning is an important routine job for Israeli women soldiers.

66. Sergeant-Major Flora Sandes, who fought in the front line in the Serbian Army.

SOLDIERS OF
MANY LANDS

167. A new recruit to the Pontiff's Swiss Guar[d] takes the oath of allegiance to the Pope.

168. French troops have their arms and equip[-] ment inspected by an officer.

169. Elite of the Greek Army, these Evzone[s] are on parade in their picturesque uniform[s].

170. Russian infantrymen march through th[e] streets of Moscow.

A nation's history and its character are reflected in many ways in its Army—traditional corps, special uniforms and customs continue through the generations. Many countries can boast of interesting military features.

The sixteenth century uniform of the famous Swiss infantry is still worn by the Vatican Guards. These foot soldiers were first employed by Pope Julius II (1503—1513) when Switzerland probably had the finest soldiers in Europe. The Guards were originally enlisted in the canton of Lucerne, but now they are recruited from all parts of Switzerland.

Sixteenth century uniform is also worn by the Yeomen of the Guard and the Yeomen Warders of the Tower of London The uniform of both bodies of men dates from the early years of the sixteenth century, but a Guardsman can be distinguished from a Warder by a cross belt, which is not worn by the latter. Both these formations of Foot Guards are popularly known as "beefeaters", probably from the rations with which they were principally supplied. They are selected from time-expired Warrant and Non-commissioned officers of the Regular Army. The Yeomen of the Guard carry out a number of ceremonial duties, having originated as a body of men responsible for the protection of the monarch, whilst the Yeomen Warders are purely concerned with duties at the Tower of London.

Special regiments of many nations wear distinctive uniform. A number of British Highland regiments wear the kilt in the regimental tartan with Highland dress. Greek infantry from the mountains also wear a kind of kilt with a picturesque uniform. These Evzones are rifle regiments and they wear a wide skirt and tufted shoes. The Italian Bersaglieri, also rifle regiments, were founded in 1836. Their attractive uniform, with a jaunty feather in the head-dress, coupled with their fine fighting record, has won them a leading place in the Italian Army and renown the world over.

MILITARY TRADITION IN FRANCE

The *Corps d'élite* of France in the seventeenth and eighteenth centuries was the *Maison Militaire du Roi*, troops of the royal household. They always took a distinctive part in the many French wars of the period, and membership brought immense prestige. Commanders were princes of the blood, and noble-born young men sought fame, fortune or death in the ranks of the *Maison du Roi*.

Napolean I created his famous Imperial Guard, in which officers held a higher army rank than in the Guard. The general advance of the Old Guard at the Battle of Waterloo was Napoleon's last bid to save the day; its failure was his doom.

The French Foreign Legion had a special aura of toughness in more recent times. The corps was renowned for hard living, harsh discipline and hard fighting. The Legion was the last resort for desperate men of spirit of all nationalities.

The modern crack corps of France is *Les Paras*, the parachutists, who have inherited the formidable traditions of France's long military past.

RUSSIAN GUARDS

The Russian revolution of 1917 brought a complete break with the traditions, names and customs of the Tzarist army, though the nature of some of the corps is unchanged. The skill and prowess of the Cossack cavalry is centuries old. New distinctions were created in World War II, when a number of regiments were named Guards in recognition of outstanding achievements, such as the Panfilov Guards of the Battle of Moscow.

U.S. MARINES

The United States Marine Corps is known the world over. It was formed in 1775, at the outbreak of the war between Britain and her American colonists. Two battalions were raised to aid the defence of the colonies and they were modelled in organisation, drill and dress on the British infantry of the time. The U.S. Marines became a military organisation, complete in itself, which also formed an integral part of the American Naval service. The Marines have taken a prominent part in every war in which America has been engaged, and they particularly distinguished themselves fighting the Japanese in the Pacific theatre during World War II.

THE JAPANESE SAMURAI

Japan has a long and very strong military tradition, which was based for centuries on an hereditary military officer caste, the *Samurai*. The *Samurai* were dedicated to the profession of arms, scorned to follow any other calling, and lived their lives to a strict and spartan code. Manliness was everything, with simplicity of living, frugality, self-discipline and reverence for ancestors. If a *Samurai* erred or broke the strict rules of his code, suicide (or *harakiri*) was his only course—death on his sword.

Samurai weapons were the sword and the bow. The sword was the finest the world has ever seen, the only kind to surpass the magnificent Spanish blades of Toledo. The bow was very large and powerful, and was used on horseback. The grip was a third of the bow's length from the bottom, and the arrows, like those of the English longbow, were a yard long.

The armour worn by the *Samurai* was quite distinctive, and unlike any worn in Europe. Cuirass, helmet of unusual and ornate design, face mask, mail-and-plate-covered fabric sleeves and shin guards were joined by brightly-coloured cords. The metal was brilliantly inlaid with gold or silver. *Samurai* armour was extremely ornate and colourful and, until the fifteenth century, the shoulder guards, hip and stomach guards, and thigh guards like aprons, were suspended so that the human form was hidden behind a colourful and complicated pattern of iron and cloth; long veils of coloured silk were attached as well. After the fifteenth century, a lighter and simpler armour was worn, but it was still highly decorative.

The *Samurai* were abolished towards the end of the nineteenth century, but their spirit was in some measure preserved among Japanese officers. In World War II, Japanese pilots dived their aircraft into their targets, purposely destroying themselves to make sure of their objective. There were also examples of Japanese officers committing *harakiri* on their swords.

MILITARY ACADEMIES

The efficiency and success of an army depends to a considerable degree on the quality and ability of its officers. Military academies for training cadets receive special attention, and the training is always hard, directed towards forming character as well as acquiring military knowledge.

The French *Ecole Spéciale Militaire* at St Cyr, near Versailles, was founded by Napoleon in 1808. The two principal British military academies are older: The Royal Military Academy, Woolwich, was founded in 1741, and the Royal Military College, Sandhurst, in 1802.

The year 1802 is also the date of the foundation of the United States Military Academy at West Point, some fifty miles north of New York. West Point was a site of great strategic importance in the American War of Independence, as it controlled the valley of the River Hudson. General

171. Warlike charge of North Africa's Sp
mounted warriors.

172. Swiss machine-gunner in action dur
winter manoeuvres in the Bernese Oberla

173. Musicians of Italy's famous Bersagl
play their instruments whilst running,
ceremonial occasions.

172

173

174. Italian gunners enjoy a meal during the course of field exercises.

175. Companions in arms, an American and a German soldier discuss the workings of an M 48 tank.

176. A corporal of the Luxembourg Army briefs his men before an exercise.

177. Greek infantry prepare to repulse an imminent attack.

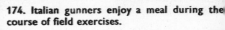

TOP: Trooping the Colour ceremony on Horse Guards Parade, London.

BOTTOM LEFT: Chelsea Pensioners celebrating Oak Apple Day in the traditional manner.

BOTTOM RIGHT: The Goat Major with Taffy, proud mascot of The Welsh Regiment.

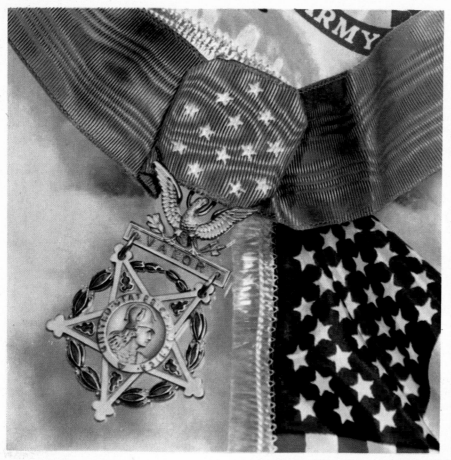

ABOVE: The Congressional Medal of Honor — the American Army's highest award.

ABOVE RIGHT: The Croix de Guerre — the premier military honour in France.

BELOW: The Victoria Cross — the British award for the very highest feats of valour.

178. An armoured-car unit of the Jordan Army parades with its colour and falcon mascot.

179. Cadets at Turkey's tough Kuleli Military College marching to take over guard duty.

180. International parade. The detachments in this picture represent, from left to right: Canada, Belgium, Germany, Turkey, United Kingdom, Portugal, The Netherlands, France, Norway, Luxembourg, Italy, Iceland, Greece, United States and Denmark.

Washington had his headquarters there for a few months in 1779. Washington urged that West Point should become a military academy in 1796, and six years later his wish was fulfilled.

West Point cadets are put through a most rigorous four-year period of training, and their first twelve months are particularly tough. Distinctive uniforms are worn, some of which derive from the eighteenth century.

The Soviet Army's oldest school—The Frunze Military Academy—graduates army commanders, and Russia also possesses a number of special academies for the purpose of training officers for the various branches: artillery, armour, engineers, signals, and so on. In addition, there is an academy in Moscow which provides courses for General Staff officers.

181

181. Moorish Guard of the Spanish Army.

182. Amongst the finest mountain troops the world are these Alpini of the Italian Arm

183. France also boasts some very fine troc specially trained for mountain warfare.

183

182

SOLDIERS
OF THE
COMMONWEALTH

184

The British Commonwealth of Nations is a free association of independent sovereign states, of different races, religions and traditions, linked by common ideals. This was clearly shown by the fact that the nations of the Commonwealth fought side by side during both World Wars, though for many of them the causes of the wars were as remote as the enemy. Each Commonwealth army has its own particular customs and traditions, and each has its own pride of achievement. It is only possible to mention a few such achievements here, a selection of many famous corps and great exploits.

THE SOLDIERS OF CANADA

The Canadian Regiment of Guards has a long history, and like their prototypes in Britain, they are famed in ceremonial drill. Organised along the lines of the British footguards, they wear scarlet jackets and bearskins for ceremonial parade, and have the highest traditions both as fighting troops and masters of drill.

In World War I, the Canadian divisions which fought in France throughout the long years of trench warfare crowned their many achievements by making the initial attack on the German line in 1918, the attack which led to the final break-through and the German surrender. The stretch of German trenches which the Canadian Corps attacked in August, 1918, was one of the most formidable of the whole German line. Nevertheless, after eight days the 1st, 2nd and 3rd Canadian Divisions, together with the 51st (British) Division, fought through and forced the Germans to fall back from the Somme, the scene of so much murderous fighting in the previous four years. The success led directly to the massive Allied attack on the Hindenburg Line and the final victory in France.

The gallant raid on Dieppe in World War II was made by a predominantly Canadian force. Hitler's fortress of Europe was still intact, and the

185

186

185. Australian infantrymen receiving exper
arms instruction.

186. Indian troops in action.

187. A unit of the Trucial Oman Scouts pre
pares to depart on desert patrol.

188. This Gurkha soldier, serving with th
British Army, is presenting his curved, razo
sharp kukri for inspection.

187

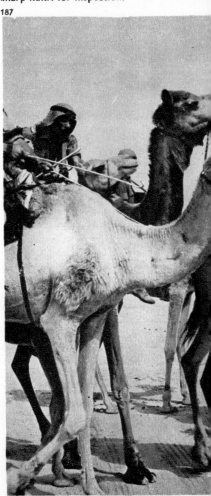

brilliant raid on St Nazaire in March, 1942, had increased the vigilance of
the Germans. The raid on Dieppe was made in August, 1942, by a force
of 5,000, with the object of causing as much damage as possible to the
harbour installations and of creating the maximum alarm in the enemy
camp. Another object was to gain information for mounting the invasions
which would follow at a later date.

The assault troops met with tremendous defensive fire, and the opposition
was much stronger than had been expected. The attack was pressed home,
however, with the greatest gallantry, although the losses were appalling.
Of the 5,000 troops, nearly 1,000 were killed and 2,000 taken prisoner.
The raid was largely a failure, but the sacrifice was not made in vain.
It provided information of the highest value, and helped to make the in-
vasion of Sicily successful eleven months later, an invasion in which the
Canadians also played a vital part.

AUSTRALIA AND NEW ZEALAND

The story of the Australian and New Zealand troops—the Anzacs—at
Gallipoli, in 1915, has already been told, and it is commemorated annually
on Anzac Day. In World War II, the Anzacs showed that they had inherited all the traditions of fine fighting men from their fathers. They were
engaged in European campaigns, and in the Far East against Japan.

In the autumn of 1942, the Japanese had invaded New Guinea and
were within twenty miles of Port Moresby, on the threshold of Australia.
The 6th and 7th Divisions of the Australian Imperial Forces marched over
the Owen Stanley Mountains and, with their American allies, threw the
Japanese back, cleared New Guinea and removed the threat of an invasion
of Australia.

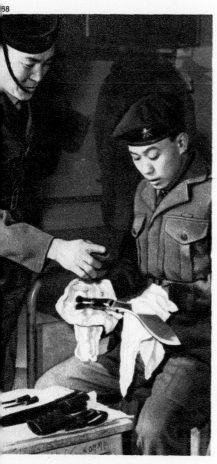

In Europe, the Australians had the right of the British line at the Battle of El Alamein in October, 1942; 30 Corps, on the right of the Eighth Army, was a Commonwealth Corps. The five divisions consisted of the 51st (British) Division, the 2nd New Zealand, the 9th Australian, the 4th Indian and the 1st South African.

The Australians swung right-handed towards the coast and attacked the very strong German positions, fighting their way through and isolating the German left flank. The New Zealand Division was entrusted with the vital task of driving a wedge through the enemy line, so that the armoured divisions could move forward through the gap they created.

THE BRITISH GUARDS

The British Household Cavalry and the Brigade of Guards are the senior regiments in the British Army. The Life Guards and the Royal Horse Guards, which together constitute the Household Cavalry, are the Sovereign's personal bodyguard. Both regiments were formed in 1661. The Life Guards wear scarlet tunics with blue collars and cuffs, and a white plume on their helmets, when in full dress. The Royal Horse Guards, known also by their ancient title of The Blues, wear blue tunics with red collars and cuffs, and a red plume. Both wear polished-steel breastplates and knee-high riding boots. The Household Cavalry provide the escort for state occasions, and two mounted troopers are on sentry duty by day outside The Horseguards, in Whitehall, providing one of the traditional sights of London.

The Brigade of Guards consists of five regiments: the Grenadier Guards, the Coldstream Guards, the Scots Guards, the Irish Guards and the Welsh Guards. In full dress, the Guards wear scarlet tunics and bearskin caps. Typical of the details of dress dear to most regiments, they have various arrangements of the tunic buttons, and wear different plumes in their bearskins. The buttons of the Grenadiers are spaced equally and their plume is white, worn on the left side of the bearskin. The buttons of the Coldstream Guards are in pairs, and a red plume is worn on the right of the bearskin. The Scots Guards have their buttons in groups of three and no plume. The Irish Guards have their buttons in sets of four and a blue plume, and the Welsh Guards have the buttons in fives, with a green and white plume.

Troops of these five regiments are usually responsible for mounting guard on Buckingham Palace and other royal palaces. On the Sovereign's official birthday, a battalion of the Guards has the honour of Trooping the Colour, while the Household Cavalry provide the royal mounted escort. The Guards are famous the world over for the precision of their ceremonial drill, and for their magnificent record as fighting men.

INDIA AND PAKISTAN

In the days before the independence of India and Pakistan, the British Army learned to respect and admire the soldiers of the sub-continent, both as a hard-fighting foe and as loyal and reliable troops within the Indian Army. There are many famous regiments, such as the Bengal Lancers, renowned for their skill in battle and their prowess on the polo ground. All the regiments of cavalry and infantry, drawn from every province, have their own characteristics and their honoured place in military history. The large number of V.C.s won by the soldiers of India and Pakistan in the two world wars is a measure of their quality.

The Gurkha regiments still serve with the British Army. They come from Nepal, an independent Himalayan State between India and Tibet, and they are traditionally cheerful, hardy, self-reliant soldiers renowned as superb shots. Magnificent in close fighting, the Gurkhas use their heavy curved knives (kukris) with deadly effect. Alongside the regiments from India and Pakistan, Gurkhas fought with great distinction in both the world wars.

The Sikh soldiers proved their quality in the two Sikh wars of 1845 and 1848, when the British Army found that their cavalry, infantry and artillery were skilled, fierce fighters. Later generations of Sikhs, serving with the British Army in India, maintained the tradition. They fought with great distinction at Neuve Chapelle and the Second Battle of Ypres in World War I, and against the Japanese in World War II.

Even a brief account of the soldiers of India and Pakistan would take many pages. Since the British left India, the regiments of both nations continue to maintain their reputation of being among the best disciplined and finest soldiers in the world.

189. Gunners of the King's African Rifles fire a salute in Mauritius.

190. Ghanaian Presidential guardsman.

THE SOLDIERS OF AFRICA

Africa does not, like India, have a long tradition of military service, but the two world wars proved that, when he is properly trained and has good officers, the African becomes a splendid fighting man.

A fine example is provided by the King's African Rifles, recruited from Kenya, Uganda and Tanganyika; twenty-two battalions were raised in World War I. Pride of corps is nourished by tradition, and every African regiment can look back on good and honourable service in the campaigns of the twentieth century.

MEDALS FOR BRAVERY

Special medals have been struck and presented to individuals by sovereigns at various times in history, but it did not become the regular practice to award medals to soldiers until the beginning of the nineteenth century. Queen Elizabeth I of England struck a special medal in 1588 to commemorate the defeat of the Spanish Armada, but the distribution was not general. The Honourable East India Company was the first to bestow medals on officers and men alike, after a campaign towards the end of the eighteenth century.

The first regular award was made by the British Government in the Peninsular War. In 1810, the practice was instituted of awarding a gold medal to officers of the rank of battalion commander and above after a successful battle. If an officer was due to receive more than one, he had a gold clasp on the medal ribbon for each subsequent award. The first medal to be generally awarded to all ranks, the same for officers and men, was the Waterloo Medal of 1815, which was suggested by the Duke of Wellington. After that, the award of campaign medals became general, with a clasp for each battle.

Campaign medals were followed by medals conferred for personal bravery or distinguished service. The medal ribbons on the tunic of a soldier who has seen active service are arranged in a definite order, medals awarded for personal gallantry coming first, with the highest in rank nearest to the tunic buttons. A senior commander usually receives awards from his allies, and that is why a general's tunic is often ablaze with several rows of coloured ribbons.

THE CONGRESSIONAL MEDAL OF HONOR

The highest decoration conferred for bravery by the United States is the Congressional Medal of Honor. It is presented by the President in the

name of Congress to men who have risked their lives to perform some act of outstanding bravery in the presence of the enemy, above and beyond the call of duty. The award is made by a vote in Congress.

The first award was made to General Washington in 1776 for recapturing Boston from the British Army. It has always been reserved for outstanding deeds of valour. The medal is a five-pointed star in rose gold, hung from a blue silk ribbon decorated with thirteen stars. The medal is attached to the ribbon by a gold eagle and a bar on which is inscribed the single word—VALOR.

THE LEGION OF HONOUR

Napoleon instituted the Legion of Honour in 1802—a white enamel and gold badge with ten points, each tipped with a silver ball, all within a wreath of oak and laurel. There are five divisions: *Grand Croix*, *Grands Officiers*, *Commandeurs*, *Officiers* and *Chevaliers*. The Grand Cross of the Legion of Honour is the premier order of France, and is only conferred for outstanding gallantry in action or for twenty years' distinguished service.

THE VICTORIA CROSS

There are several medals awarded for gallantry or distinguished service in the British Army, but the highest of all is, of course, the Victoria Cross. The cross itself is very simple, a bronze cross with the royal crown in the centre surmounted by a lion, and the two words FOR VALOUR. The ribbon is crimson, with a small replica of the cross on it.

The V.C. was founded by Queen Victoria in 1856, after the Crimean War, and the crosses were made from the metal of captured Russian guns. It is only awarded for exceptional personal bravery in the presence of the enemy. In 1902, posthumous award of the medal was authorised and, if the man who wins it is killed, the cross is presented to his next of kin. The V.C. takes precedence over all other honours and awards, and a holder adds the letters V.C. after his name.

HERO OF THE SOVIET UNION

The highest award for bravery in the Russian Army is the title "Hero of the Soviet Union", established in 1934. It is bestowed for "individual or collective service to the country, linked with the performance of an act of heroism". The Heroes of the Soviet Union are awarded the Order of Lenin and the Gold Star medal, a five-pointed star in gold.

Individuals who win the title twice are awarded a second Gold Star, and a bronze bust with a fitting inscription is set up in their home town. A third feat of heroism wins a third Gold Star.

THE GERMAN KNIGHT'S CROSS

The Knight's Cross, with golden oak leaves, swords and diamonds, is the highest award for gallantry in the German Army. It is a black Maltese cross with silver edges, and the black, white and red ribbon is attached by a pair of gold crossed swords, with a diamond between them and a cluster of oak leaves in gold. The cross was instituted in 1944 as an award for repeated exceptional gallantry, or repeated exceptional merit in operational and military leadership.

194. The Distinguished Service Medal and ribbon, obverse (U. K., 1914).

195. The Order of Lenin and ribbon, obverse (U. S. S. R.).

196. The Iron Cross (Prussia, 1870, showing various classes).

197. Battledress tunic of Field-Marshal Auchinleck, displaying his medal ribbons.

COLOURS AND CUSTOMS

The Roman legions had their Eagles, the symbol of the spirit of the legion, and Napoleon's regiments were led into battle by eagle standards, too. But the more common symbol was a flag or banner, in the colours and bearing the device of the commander. The flag was borne at the commander's side, to indicate the headquarters and to provide a rallying point in battle. In the old days, an army in line of battle was pricked out with colour from the many flags. The higher the rank, the larger the flag, the greatest and finest of all being the standard of the commander-in-chief, often a king or prince.

REGIMENTAL COLOURS

In the course of time, the flags came to be called Colours, from the diversity of colour they presented. When standing armies came into being, first every company, and then only every regiment, possessed Colours—in Britain, the King's Colour and the Regimental Colour. They were always carried by the youngest officers, often lads in their teens. They were the symbols of the heart and soul of a regiment, and thus were highly-prized trophies; to capture your enemy's Colours was proof positive of victory. By the same token, to lose your own was proof of defeat, so men fought to the last round to preserve their Colours and save them from falling into the hands of their adversaries.

If the Colour-bearer fell, there was always someone to take his place; there are, in fact, records of six or more successive bearers carrying the Colours in a hard-fought battle. Held high and pointing forward, the Colours were always in the van of an advance; when things went ill, they were the rallying point in the smoke and confusion of battle.

The Worcestershire Regiment cherishes the memory of two gallant young

98. The 14th Century standard of William Montagu, Earl of Salisbury.

99. Standards in use at the time of Henry VIII.

127

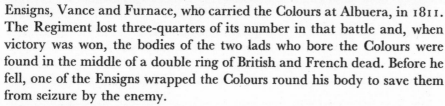

Ensigns, Vance and Furnace, who carried the Colours at Albuera, in 1811. The Regiment lost three-quarters of its number in that battle and, when victory was won, the bodies of the two lads who bore the Colours were found in the middle of a double ring of British and French dead. Before he fell, one of the Ensigns wrapped the Colours round his body to save them from seizure by the enemy.

It is a long time now since Colours were carried into battle, but every infantry regiment still has its Queen's Colour and its Regimental Colour. When Colours are renewed, the old ones are laid up in cathedrals and churches, protected by fine netting, to hang, often torn by shot, as mute testimony to battles of long ago.

TROOPING THE COLOUR

It was once the custom to march the Colours slowly along the ranks before a battle, to make sure that every soldier would recognise them in the stress and confusion of action. This is the ceremony of Trooping the Colour, performed on important regimental occasions, and by a battalion of the Guards on Horseguards Parade on the Sovereign's official birthday.

The Colour is borne by a junior officer, with an armed Colour Guard of Sergeants and, as in the old days, it is carried down the ranks at the slow march.

BATTLE HONOURS

As campaign medals are awarded to soldiers, so are Battle Honours awarded to regiments, to be embroidered on the Colours. Battle Honours before World War I are emblazoned on the Regimental Colour, subse-

200. U.S. troops raising the 'Stars and Stripes' on Mount Suribachi, Iwo Jima.

201. A Czech colour-party on the Russian front during the Second World War.

202. Colour and escort of a unit of the French Foreign Legion.

203. The culminating point in the 'backbadge' parade of the 1st Battalion Gloucestershire Regiment is reached with Trooping the Colour.

quent ones on the Queen's Colour. So many were gained in the two world wars that regiments had to make a selection for the Colours.

REGIMENTAL CUSTOMS

As Colours are a tangible representation of a regiment's entity, and the battle honours a record of its service, so do regimental traditions and customs keep its past alive. Every regiment has some special memory which is passed on to new generations by custom.

The Gloucestershire Regiment has the unique privilege of wearing a badge at the back of the cap as well as in front, a reminder of the gallantry of the 28th Foot—which later became the 1st Battalion the Gloucestershire Regiment—at the Battle of Alexandria, in 1801. The 28th Foot was hotly engaged in battle with the French, when it was suddenly attacked in the rear by an enemy detachment which had penetrated the British line. The rear rank of the 28th turned about, and fought off the enemy front and rear. To commemorate this feat the regiment was authorised to wear the back badge, a sphinx and the word "Egypt" in a laurel wreath.

THE MINDEN REGIMENTS

Six British regiments commemorate the Battle of Minden on August 1st every year. They are the Suffolk Regiment (now the 1st East Anglian Regiment), the Lancashire Fusiliers, the Royal Welch Fusiliers, the King's Own Scottish Borderers, the Royal Hampshire Regiment and the King's Own Yorkshire Light Infantry.

The feat which the Minden regiments celebrate annually was an epic

129

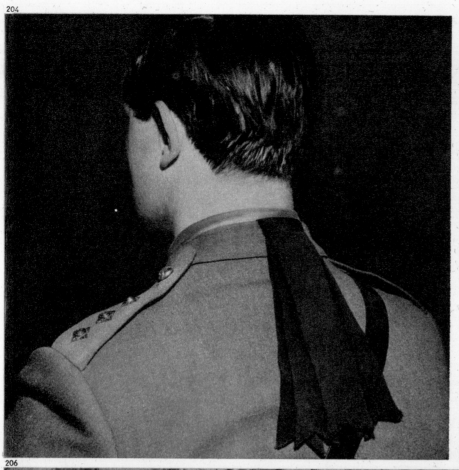

indeed. Through a mistaken order the six regiments, which were brigaded together, advanced to the sound of their drums on the massed ranks of French cavalry. Unsupported by cavalry or artillery the six regiments advanced steadily through murderous cross-fire of cannon and musket, suffering terrible losses but never checking their stately pace. They charged the French cavalry with the bayonet, broke the first line, re-formed, charged again and broke the second, finally scattering the enemy completely.

The six regiments lost 78 officers and 1,300 other ranks out of a total strength of 4,300, but their sublime feat won the day. As they marched to the battlefield on August 1st, 1759, the soldiers picked roses from the gardens of Minden, and put them in their hats. That is why the men of the Minden regiments wear roses on Minden Day. The Colour is hung with a wreath of roses when it is trooped, and the drums and the drum-major's staff are garlanded with roses.

The five cavalry regiments which made the charge of the Light Brigade on October 25th, 1854, keep Balaclava Day as a holiday. Many regiments have similar anniversaries, marked with a ceremonial parade in the morning, sporting events in the afternoon and a special dinner in the evening.

But regimental customs are not always derived from epic feats in battle; much less important incidents and events are commemorated. The Royal Welch Fusiliers wear a black silk ribbon attached to the back of the collar. This used to be worn by all soldiers, to protect the tunic from the grease of the short pigtail of hair which was worn. When, in 1808, an order was issued to abolish the pigtail, the 23rd Foot was at sea and did not receive it. The pigtails were cut off in due course, but the black ribbon was retained, and is still worn in commemoration of the regiment's unwitting retention of the pigtail after the rest of the Army had given it up.

04. A captain of the Royal Welch Fusiliers wearing the 'black ribbons' of his regiment.

05. Adjutant Major J. Swinton, of the Scots Guards, follows tradition by riding up the steps at the Royal Military Academy, Sandhurst.

06. A fine example of the preservation of traditional uniform for ceremonial purposes is presented by the King's Guard, in Copenhagen.

REGIMENTAL MASCOTS

Eight regiments in the British Army are recognised officially as being authorised to possess an animal mascot. The Royal Welch Fusiliers and the Welsh Regiment both have a goat; the Sherwood Foresters have a ram; The Royal Warwickshire Fusiliers have an antelope; the Argyll and Sutherland Highlanders have a Shetland pony; the Parachute Regiment has a pony for each of the three battalions; the Irish Guards have a wolf-hound; and the Queen's Own Hussars have a drum horse.

The Royal Welch Fusiliers had a goat as mascot in 1775, during the American War, and the Welsh Regiment acquired its goat in India during the First Afghan campaign of 1839–1842. The Sherwood Foresters got their first ram in India, too, in 1838. It was called Derby, and the name has been given to every regimental ram since. It was while they were in India that the Royal Warwickshire Fusiliers acquired their first antelope, in 1871.

When the regimental mascot parades on ceremonial occasions it is always carefully groomed; hooves are polished, and a splendid jacket and collar is worn. Sometimes the horns are tipped with silver.

Mascots, details of dress, badges, special marches, different ways of honouring the royal toast and a host of other traditions are all precious to a regiment or corps. Titles may change and regiments become amalgamated, but time-honoured customs are carefully preserved. The rank and file are always changing, but through every succeeding generation the spirit and character of each regiment remains the same, its past firmly linked to the present by the unbreakable bonds of tradition and custom.

131

MODEL
SOLDIERS

In the tomb of an Egyptian prince who died more than four thousand years ago archaeologists found model soldiers among the treasures buried with him—soldiers made of wood and painted. The Romans made model soldiers, and doubtless they were as meticulous over details of uniform and weapons as the model-makers of today. The Emperor Maximilian used to play with model knights in armour, and King Louis XIV of France had exquisite replicas in miniature made of the *Maison du Roi*, companies of foot and troops of horse, for the young princes. They were made in Germany and cost £ 30,000 the set. There is, in fact, a long and illustrious history to the model soldier.

THE POPULARITY OF TOY SOLDIERS

Toy-makers began to produce metal model soldiers in Germany during the wars of Frederick the Great, and they became popular playthings. The idea spread, and lead soldiers became popular everywhere; varieties increased and the details were improved. They reached the height of their popularity in Britain during the second half of the nineteenth century, and shops provided an exciting variety. They sold soldiers in the uniforms of various regiments: foot soldiers in red; Scottish regiments in Highland dress; dragoons; hussars and lancers; artillery with their guns and limbers, and the horses to draw them; generals on horseback with their staff officers and the Colours in the hands of a Colour-bearer; stretcher-bearers with their stretchers; nurses; tents; wounded soldiers with bandaged heads; two-horse wagons; and full bands. The bands were always exciting, with the big drum and the kettle-drums, the different instruments, and the grand Drum-major wielding his splendid staff.

Boys could hold a parade, with every soldier in his proper place; alternatively they could stage mock battles, with the troops cunningly deployed, marbles used as ammunition, and special rules in operation about advancing, say, six inches at a time. Sir Winston Churchill related that, when he was a boy, he spent a great deal of time fighting battles with his toy soldiers, re-enacting the victories of his great ancestor, the Duke of Marlborough.

The model soldiers of the pre-khaki age were more colourful, but the modern specimens, often made of plastic, are in advance of the older types in some ways. They are also stronger; it was distressingly easy for a leaden guardsman to lose his head through an accident. Nowadays, models of weapons and vehicles are strictly to scale, and usually very accurate in detail. You can buy a wide range of modern pieces of artillery, some of which fire miniature shells, and there is a dazzling selection of tanks, armoured cars, lorries, and other equipment essential to modern warfare.

COLLECTING MODEL SOLDIERS

Model soldiers have long ceased to be only toys. It has been estimated that there are about 100,000 serious collectors in the world, most of whom are members of model soldier societies. It is a hobby which appeals to the connoisseur and historian, and the number of enthusiasts is increasing.

Collectors of model soldiers usually specialise in a period, an army, or a single regiment. A man may collect the British Army of Wellington's day, or the French of Napoleon's. He might specialise in Highlanders or concentrate on some particular regiment, his specimens recording the changes in uniform throughout its history. One collector has a set of more than 6,000 British soldiers of the nineteenth century, including a complete infantry battalion, 60 men to a company, with all the N.C.Os and officers,

7. War in miniature. This diorama portrays clash between American and British forces Bladensburg, in 1814.

8. General Lee at Gettysburg, following the onfederate defeat.

9. A group of model soldiers in uniforms of e Napoleonic era.

0. Perfect miniature representation of a andard-bearer with sword upraised.

the band, hospital orderlies, nurses, tents, and wagons for the baggage on the march.

Some collectors modify their specimens themselves, altering details with infinite skill and patience, and repainting them to produce the uniforms they want. Such enthusiasts consult libraries and military museums to ensure that every detail is correct.

MILITARY DIORAMAS

You can often see beautiful model soldiers in military and regimental museums which sometimes possess dioramas—large model presentations of a battle. The background scenery is painted, the ground features are faithfully reproduced, and the troops are deployed as they were at a certain moment in the battle. Uniforms are, of course, correctly reproduced. Puffs of cotton wool indicate gunfire, and the Colours show the position of headquarters and commanders. Model soldiers for the purpose of dioramas are often flat—two-dimensional instead of three-dimensional—but both sides in the conflict are portrayed with extreme accuracy.

A diorama of the Battle of Waterloo, formerly on show at the Royal United Services Institute in London, contained 150,000 figures, and every detail of the actual battlefield was reproduced perfectly.

The world of model soldiers never fails to fascinate people of all ages and nationalities. From the cheap toy soldier, bearing the scars of many campaigns in miniature, to the expensive, perfect replica in the prized collection of a connoisseur, these models bring pleasure to millions.

211. Bitter fighting on the beach at Tarawa depicted in diorama form.

211

THE SOLDIER'S LIFE

A soldier is a trained fighting man, skilled in the use of his weapons, sure of himself and his comrades. The recruit is drilled for long hours on the barrack square to teach him to react quickly to orders, to give him confidence and to instil the sense of discipline. Discipline raises morale; it welds individuals into a unit and makes it a fighting force.

The Drill Masters of the Roman Army saw to it that their men were trained to march, manoeuvre and bear themselves like soldiers. The Roman soldier was disciplined and tough, and for more than five centuries he was invincible.

Roman infantry exercised by marching ten miles in full equipment, alternating between marching and trotting. The Roman soldier was a professional, and he was trained to be tough and hard. In the reign of Nero, a Roman general took over an army stationed in Syria and found that it had "gone soft" through living in comfortable billets. The general promptly marched the army out of town into the bleak uplands for the winter. Many men died, and sentries were frozen to death at their posts, but when spring came the survivors won a brilliant and campaign.

When the modern recruit grumbles at the apparent senselessness of hours spent on the parade ground "square-bashing", he can take comfort from the fact that he is doing the same as soldiers right through the ages.

CONDITIONS OF SERVICE

In the Roman Army, a soldier served for a definite period; under Augustus it was for sixteen years, with four in addition as a "veteran" excused fatigues. At the end, he received a grant of land or, at some periods, a cash payment instead. There was always a cash bonus for all ranks when a new emperor was enthroned, to encourage loyalty for the new regime.

The precise contract of service did not come into use until comparatively

2. Roman soldiers escorting prisoners after battle (detail from a Roman carving).

3. Soldiers looting their defeated enemies (painting by Sebastian Vranx).

214. Foot inspection after a route-march.

215. Orders for the day being issued to cade at St Cyr, French Military Academy.

216. A squad moves at the double on a nin mile speed march.

recently. In Medieval days, soldiers were enrolled for a campaign and turned loose when it was over, with no grant of cash or pension, and sometimes without receiving the arrears of pay due to them. Discharged soldiers often became "rogues and vagabonds" living as best they could, or banding together to use their erstwhile military skill to live lawlessly.

Even when standing armies came into being in the seventeenth century, there was rarely any specific contract of service. A man served until he was discharged through age or injury, or until his regiment was disbanded. It was not until the nineteenth century that a definite length of service was established, a certain number of years with the Colours and another in the Reserve. In the two world wars, very large armies had to be mustered and civilians were enrolled "for the duration of the war".

SOLDIERS' PAY

The pay of the lowest rank of Roman soldier seems to have been about sixpence a day, and it is estimated that he could live on two-thirds of that, with the balance for the pleasures of the canteen. There were compulsory saving schemes organised on a unit basis.

Regular pay is essential for a soldier's morale, and the wise officer sees to it that his men get their due pay on the proper day; but for centuries soldiers' pay was badly managed, and was more often than not in arrears. In 1346, an English foot soldier received 3d. a day; in 1415—the year of Agincourt—it was 6d., and in 1557 it had been raised to 8d. It eventually became 1/—a day, and remained at that until the nineteenth century. Deductions were made to cover clothing, messing and other items.

The modern soldier is paid regularly and meticulously, and careful accounts are kept on his behalf, in the British Army by the Royal Army Pay Corps. A soldier's pay is managed in an enlightened manner; it is realised that he deserves a reasonable wage, and additional pay is awarded for extra skill and proficiency. Family allowances are paid and, at the end of a sufficient length of service, a pension for life.

DISCIPLINE AND PUNISHMENT

Discipline in the Roman Army was severe, and so were the punishments. Mutiny, or desertion in the face of the enemy, was punished by death. If a unit mutinied or deserted in action, it was paraded, and every tenth man was executed. For allowing the enemy to break into his camp and set fire to it, Mark Antony executed every tenth man of the two units concerned, dismissed their commanders and put the remainder on half rations. A sentry found asleep at his post was stoned to death by his comrades. If a deserter was recaptured, his right hand was struck off. Flogging, reductions in pay and half-rations were frequent punishments.

Savage punishments continued in subsequent armies. As with the Romans, mutiny or desertion in action meant death, the most drastic punishment being used to deter others. Until only a hundred years ago soldiers, and sailors as well, were punished harshly. Up to the beginning of the nineteenth century, men were flogged at the halberds, their wrists lashed to the top of a tripod. They were also made to run the gauntlet, through a double rank of men armed with bayonet scabbards or sticks.

Floggings were in public and were accompanied by the roll of drums, and sentences were up to 500 lashes. It was a matter of pride not to permit a groan or whimper to pass the lips. A deserter who was recaptured was

branded with the letter "D" on the wrist after he had been punished.

Military law and punishment has, like all else concerning the life of the soldier, become enlightened. The punishments which can be awarded by a commanding officer or a court-martial are very carefully defined. A soldier's hard-won rights are as jealously guarded as those of a civilian.

PRISONERS OF WAR

The treatment of prisoners of war always depended on their rank. An officer was looked upon as a possible source of ransom, and for that reason he was usually treated well, but the "other ranks" usually became slaves; the Romans used them at the oars of their galleys or as slave labour. The system continued through the Middle Ages; common prisoners were either killed forthwith or used for slave labour.

It was somewhat different in siege warfare. Prisoners of rank were treated as guests, and others were either sent away or, more likely, hanged from the ramparts, because their captors did not want extra mouths to feed.

The ransom money to be obtained for well-born prisoners was considered one of the perquisites of war and a useful source of profit. King Richard I of England, captured by Leopold of Austria in 1192 on his way back from the Crusade, was ransomed for the record price of 150,000 marks.

The treatment of prisoners of war was controlled by the Hague War Regulations of 1899. By these it was internationally agreed that prisoners of war must be treated humanely, and that their food, clothing and quarters must be the same as for the troops of the country who had captured them. Prisoners may be made to work, but not officers. The work must not in any way assist military operations, it must not be excessive, and it must be paid for at the rate which the captor's own troops would receive.

217. Pay parade for the Scots Guards.

218. Sport plays a large part in the life of modern soldier.

19. Prisoners of War in the 20th Century can generally expect infinitely better treatment than their predecessors in former times.

20. Inoculation is just one of the many medical precautions taken by military authorities to protect the soldier of today.

ESCAPERS

A prisoner's instinct is to escape if he can, and there are always bold spirits who will make the attempt. There were many daring escapes during the two world wars. Some men broke out and were recaptured several times, eventually succeeding in their attempts despite the fact that they were confined in special, heavily-guarded prisons for persistent escapers.

The wooden horse escape of Eric Williams from a German prison camp in World War II is famous. The prisoners made a wooden vaulting horse from packing cases and put it in the compound. The German guards watched the prisoners using the horse for exercises. Underneath, however, the tunnelling party was at work. Eric Williams and two companions got out and made their way across Germany to Sweden, and so to England.

To get on the other side of the wire is only the beginning of an escaper's problems. He must have procured, or made, inconspicuous clothing and kept it hidden in the camp. He must have identity papers, money and a map. Then he has to make his way through hostile territory and cross the frontier. Of the hundreds of escape plans which were made, only a small proportion succeeded, and of those who did escape from prison camps, only a few managed to escape from the enemy country.

Special escape kits were issued in World War II to men on missions which might lead to their capture. These included a map—sometimes printed on a silk handkerchief—and a compass, in a collar stud or a button.

THE INTERNATIONAL RED CROSS

Regulations governing the care of the sick and wounded in war were agreed at the important Geneva Convention of 1906. By this it was recognised that ambulances and military hospitals, their medical and administrative staffs, and chaplains, are to be "respected and protected under all circumstances". The sign that this protection is demanded is the red cross, on a flag, sign or arm-band. The Red Cross organisation is equally concerned with caring for a wounded man whether he be friend or foe. Parcels of food, clothing or comforts for prisoners of war sent by the Red Cross, or other recognised organisations, are, by international agreement, to be delivered by the nation holding the prisoners.

The Red Cross can, of course, play only a non-combatant part in any war; wearers of the badge never carry weapons. The organisation remains neutral at all times and has one function only, to alleviate suffering.

THE SOLDIER OF ALL AGES

The soldier's life does not change in essentials. The Roman legionary, the medieval archer, the musketeer and the modern soldier all have certain essentials in common.

The soldier of Rome often served far from his home, quartered in efficient and orderly hutted camps built by the legions. The medieval soldier slept where he could, near the fine tent of the knight or lord he served. In the eighteenth century, soldiers were given billets in inns, or camped out in tents. The soldier of today has well-designed barracks, with a canteen, television and sports ground. Much is different yet much is the same; comradeship, songs to sing, rivalry between units and, always, *esprit de corps*. These were the same in armies at all times, and will never change.

COLOUR PLATES

TOP: Victor and vanquished — two miniatu[re] knights in armour.

BOTTOM: A colourful parade of model 18th Century soldiers.

221. Known as the 'skin-head', this style [of] haircut is widely used in the American force[s]

222. Religious service aboard ship, conducte[d] by a service chaplain.

221

222

ABOVE: Charge of British cavalry at the Battle of Waterloo.

BELOW: The Kaiser and his Staff.

TOP RIGHT: Handing over the Colours at a ceremonial parade held by the 1st Battalion South Staffordshire Regiment.

BOTTOM RIGHT: The U. S. Army conducts a test with the Pershing ballistic missile and the CH-47A Chinook helicopter.

THE SOLDIER OF TODAY

The strength of an army once depended on its numbers: the more men, the greater the power. Victory generally went to the big battalions, and one man represented one bullet, one bayonet, one sabre. Now it is different for, with automatic weapons and swift transportation, the whole pattern has changed. New weapons have brought a vast increase in the speed, destructive capacity, accuracy and range of fire-power. One man has the fire-power of a score in his father's day, of a hundred in his grandfather's.

These new weapons have reduced the number of men required to perform a specific task. In the British Army, for example, more than a hundred infantry regiments of two battalions each have been reduced to forty-nine regiments of one battalion each. These have been grouped into thirteen brigades of three or four battalions each; they are, in effect, thirteen regimental units. Yet the actual fire-power possessed by the new military formations, containing a fraction of the number of men required in the old, is many times greater.

BRAINS OR BRAWN?

Accompanying the reduction of numbers, there is a corresponding increase in quality. Once any man of good physique and character could be turned into a good soldier. He was asked little more than to obey orders quickly, learn his drill and weapon-training, and take his place in the ranks. Modern armies ask a great deal more; up-to-date weapons and equipment need men with technical ability and skill. Once anyone fit and willing was welcome; now only the best, physically and mentally, are good enough for the armed forces.

The old drill-sergeant used to roar: "You're not paid to think, you're paid to do as you're told!" The modern soldier *is* paid to think; he must to be able to master automatic weapons, electric and electronic equipment,

23. The Honor Guard assembles for dress inspection at Fort Myer, Virginia.

24. A Selection Board interviews a potential commissioned officer.

COLOUR PLATES

TOP: Troops of the Aden Federal Army take up a hasty position on mountain manoeuvres.

BOTTOM: Trumpeters of the Welsh Brigade sound a fanfare from the roof of their H.Q.

224

radio, and the many mechanical devices which science and the inventor have provided for him. He must be able to think for himself, be self-reliant, and show initiative.

The higher standard required in the private soldier naturally means higher standards of knowledge and skill in the N.C.O.s and officers. Soldiers, in fact, are now specialists.

THE OLD AND THE NEW

The Lifeguard or Horse Guard in his polished cuirass and plumed helmet, astride his fine horse, is a picturesque reminder of the more colourful days which have passed. So is the Guardsman in scarlet tunic and bearskin, pacing his solemn beat from his sentry box. To some people, such soldiers may appear to be out of place in a modern army, but in fact this is not the case at all.

A trooper of the Household Cavalry also wears overalls, maintains and drives an armoured car, operates its radio and uses the vehicle's automatic weapon. The scarlet-coated Guardsman spends a lot of his time in battledress, and is trained to fight with a Pritchett gun in infantry operations controlled by radio. The officer whom we see in his brilliant uniform, mounted on his splendid charger, can command a troop or squadron of armoured cars in action.

Similarly, the technically-trained infantryman, or the cavalryman trained to operate an armoured vehicle, can take part with assurance in the complicated and immaculate drill of a ceremonial parade. The old has not been forgotten in the new.

Uniform was once splendid and colourful, to foster the soldier's pride in his corps and to impress the enemy. When, however, bright-coloured coats were found to provide good targets for riflemen, drab khaki replaced the brave scarlet.

Later, the khaki tunics, with leather belts and cloth puttees, were replaced by the more comfortable and efficient battledress. That again has been modified, for there is one purpose only in the design of soldiers' dress for active service, and that is comfort combined with efficiency. Nowadays, there is a wide range of clothing available so that, wherever a soldier serves—in the tropics or the arctic, in the jungle or in snow—he will be comfortable, efficient and inconspicuous.

BOOTS, WHEELS AND WINGS

From the days when the Roman legions marched across Europe, along the straight broad roads which followed in the wake of Rome's conquests, until World War I, the soldier had to rely principally on his legs. Then began a revolution in the means of transporting soldiers over long distances. Veterans of World War I will remember the French railway wagons bearing the notice—"Horses 10, men 40". Motor transport was also used to some extent in that war, and a fleet of London motor-buses served with distinction in France.

With the development of motor transport between the wars, infantrymen were spared a great deal of marching, and motor lorries became part of the standard equipment of every unit in World War II.

After that came the age of wings, and a revolution in the mobility of troops. Troop-carrying planes can transport a battalion, a brigade or a whole division, with all its weapons and equipment, to the other side of the world in a matter of hours. Gliders and helicopters can deliver units

225.—226. Present-day duties of the Household Cavalry include both the operation of light armoured vehicles and the provision of ceremonial mounted guards for State occasions

225

to the heart of a battle, and parachute drops have become an integral part of almost all major operations.

PUSH-BUTTON SOLDIERS

The scientist and the inventor have changed the soldier's business. One problem of the twentieth-century commander has been to know exactly what is happening during a battle; the vast increase in mobility makes rapid communication essential. The field telephone was a great step forward in this direction; then came radio, with "walkie-talkie" sets to keep a forward unit in contact with headquarters. Now television is being employed, experimentally, to flash vital information to H.Q., so that there is the minimum of delay in meeting each new development in a constantly changing situation.

Technology has replaced the trained runners who carried messages to Greek and Roman commanders, the "gallopers" used by the general staff in Wellington's day, and the carrier-pigeons that helped to speed delivery of dispatches during the nineteenth century.

Gunners and infantrymen now have weapons which fire guided missiles, directing the shell on to the target. Computers are used for complicated calculations, and the magic of Radar is in general use.

Always there is something new, yet always there must be the soldier to fight, however clever the inventor may be in providing weapons and equipment. Rocket propulsion gives weapons immense range and power, but that rocket still has to be directed and controlled by a soldier, and troops are still required for mopping up after a bombardment, however devastating it may be.

Hence the specialisation of the modern soldier, the technical knowledge and skill he must possess, his long and difficult training. Nevertheless, it remains the soldier who, in the end, decides an engagement by physically occupying the enemy's territory. The soldier and his spear or bow, the musket, the rifle or the modern sub-machine gun is the final arbiter. Inventors are still busy with the rifle, and there is now a model made of aluminium and glass fibre which weighs only six pounds. Its power is such that at 500 yards the bullet will penetrate both sides of a steel helmet. It can be fired by single shots, or as an automatic weapon at the rate of 750 bullets a minute.

227. Troops testing new uniforms, specially designed for wear in hot, dry climates, where maximum protection from sand and dust is absolutely essential.

THE PROFESSION OF ARMS

There have always been men of an adventurous nature to whom the life of a soldier appeals, with its comradeship, its travel and its fundamental sense of service. Times change, weapons change, and the soldier's qualifications change with them—but the essentials do not change. Friendships, the cheerful communal life, the pattern of service routine, and the deep and often unexpressed pride in one's corps, is the same now as ever it was for those who take up the profession of arms.

Despite all the new weapons, traditions remain alive, and the modern soldier going into action—fully mindful of the deeds of his predecessors under commanders of long ago—is determined not to fail them. Unchanged, too, is the basic purpose of the soldier: to be trained and ready to fight in a just cause, so that those whom he defends may be safeguarded against invasion—with its attendant death and destruction—so that order may be preserved, and so that people may live securely and in peace.

228. 'Les Paras' dropping from aircraft over Norfolk, England, in a joint exercise with British paratroops.

229. Demonstration of water-walking by U. S. troops. Using methane foam shoes, a speed of 3 m.p.h. can be achieved.

230. 'Vigilant' anti-tank missile simulator seen in operation.

231. An American soldier on the mobile laboratory treadmill, located in the desert, is measured for body temperature at the hottest period of the day.

232. Only tents and snow-holes provide protection for troops undergoing cold-weather tests in Scotland.

233. British 'tommy' kitted out and armed for modern warfare.

ACKNOWLEDGEMENTS

Agence Rapho
Alinari
Australian News and Information Service
Australian War Memorial, Canberra
Bell, Howarth Ltd.
British Aircraft Corporation
British Museum
British Nylon Spinners
British Travel & Holidays Association
Alfred Brod Gallery, London
Camera Press Ltd
Canada House, London
Central Press Photos Ltd
Crown Copyright Reserved photographs
  by the War Office,
    Central Office of Information, and
    Ministry of Works and Public Buildings.
Corps H. Q., W. R. A. C.
Department of the Army, Washington,
  U. S. A.
Ente Provinciale Turismo, Siena
Feature-Pix
Fotokronika Tass, Moscow
Fox Photos Ltd
French Railways Ltd
John R. Freeman
Garrett Corporation, U. S. A.
Giraudon
Historisches Bildarchiv Leihweise
Michael Holford
Imperial War Museum
John Player and Sons
Keystone Press Agency Ltd
Kunstsammlung Basel

L. E. A.
Mansell Collection
Mansell (Alinari)
Mansell (Anderson)
Terence Mead
Muzeum Wojska Polskiego
National Army Museum
Norman Newton Ltd
New Zealand High Commission
North Atlantic Treaty Organisation
N. A. T. O. (Supreme Headquarters
  Allied Powers Europe)
Parker Gallery
P. A. Reuter Photos Ltd
Paul Popper Ltd
Pictorial Press Ltd
Radio Times Hulton Picture Library
Rolls Royce Ltd
Royal Armoured Corps Tank Museum
Royal Engineers Museum, Chatham
Scala
J. Scheerboom (John Baker)
Society for Cultural Relations
  with the U. S. S. R.
'Soldier', The British Army Magazine
Soviet Embassy, London
Sport and General Press Agency, Ltd
Twentieth Century Fox Film Co. Ltd
Ullstein Bilderdienst
United Press International
United States Information Service
United States Military Academy,
  West Point, New York
Victoria and Albert Museum, London
Roger Wood
Yugoslav Embassy, London

W. V. Lande fecit